I Decided To Laugh

By MJ Stroman

© 2021 MJ Stroman | I Decided to Laugh

Book Cover Design: TamikaINK.com

Interior Book Design & Formatting: TamikaINK.com

Edited by: Heather L. Duma

ISBN: 979-8-9854737-3-5

Published By: Tamika INK

Library of Congress Cataloging – in- Publication Data has been applied for.

PRINTED IN THE UNITED STATES OF AMERICA.

Dedication

I dedicate this book to all the children who were and are being abused sexually, physically, mentally, and emotionally. I wrote this book to be a voice for all those who cannot verbally explain what has happened to them or what is going on with them right now because of what they have endured. I want every boy, girl, and adult that has been a victim of sexual, mental, emotional, or physical abuse to know - it was not your fault! You are not defined by the violation you were a victim of. I pray that you will find it in your heart to forgive the person or persons who violated and abused you. That unforgiveness only turns into bitterness that will hurt you, not the person who violated you. God will handle them for every hurt that they have ever caused you. "Vengeance is mine; I will repay," says the Lord in Romans 12:35. I also dedicate this book to my three beautiful daughters LaToya, Nikki, and Lauren. You young ladies made it easy to do my assignment as a mother. You all made my assignment amazing, exciting, and fun. It is my pleasure to be your mother. This journey thus far was challenging, difficult, and even made me cry sometimes. But you all motivated and challenged me every day to be better, do better, and try harder than the day before. Your beautiful faces encouraged me to believe the words of God that I could do "all things through Christ who strengthens me!" Philippians 4:13. I love you, LaToya, Nikki, and Lauren.

Table of Contents

Introduction

L et's be clear; this is not a book to bash my mother. I am simply telling my story to educate other parents, especially single mothers. My goal is to spread awareness, educate, and get the government to make stiffer laws and rehabilitation for child sex offenders to stop the cycle of repeated sex offenders. I wanted to be candid and transparent to show the real emotions and effects that childhood trauma has on a child. I felt I needed to show the scars, the pain, and the damage that one has to mask when violated. I needed to sound the alarm to show the long-term effect of childhood trauma on a child that grows into an adult. I also wanted to acknowledge that the trauma of childhood sexual abuse, if not treated, will show up later in our adult lives. And if not treated, it will spill out on our children while we are raising them.

One of my goals for writing this book is to allow single parents, especially single mothers, to know what happened to them has not gone overlooked or unnoticed, it was not their fault, and that they can start their healing process today. I want all mothers, especially single mothers, to know that they are very important, they have the most important job on the face of the earth, and they matter. We can not change the past, but we can learn from it and reshape our future.

My mother was a great provider, and her love language was giving my sister and me the best that money could buy. My mother was not affectionate, but she loved us. My mother ruled her household with fear and an iron fist due to a father not being in the home. She did not know that having a candid conversation with her children could have worked out better than fear.

I have found as a mother that talking with my children is extremely important and very effective. Keeping it real and telling them the truth about everything with boundaries works. I spoke to my children in their language so they could understand and hear me. I tried to meet them individually where they were. My mother was doing the parenting job alone, some things fell through the cracks.

Both parents are essential because what one parent doesn't see, the other parent is supposed to see. Due to the weakness that is evident with one parent, the person who raped me, who was supposedly a friend to my mother, not a boyfriend, was able to betray her trust. Sex offenders need to be rehabilitated and incarcerated for their crimes. Sex offenders need mental help and therapy.

During my research, I found that most sex offenders were raped or molested. They either assume the role of a sex offender, or they act out with intense and uncontrollable anger. I found that some people are bitter. Rage can lead to a possible murder. The reason why sex offenders act out in rage is to prevent anyone from violating them again.

Parents need to talk to their children about sex offenders and being sexually violated. That should be a topic of conversation in the home the same way you talk about boys, girls, sex, drugs, and sex trafficking. It should also be discussed in our churches, schools, recreation centers, and even the White House. We need to teach our children that a sex offender could be in our family, a family member, a close family friend, or someone they do not know.

Single parents often work to provide for their children, and things sometimes happen on our watch that we didn't see coming. Not because we were negligent or not a good parent, but because we are focused on doing a job meant for two people. My mother was a single parent, and she did a great job. The person that raped me repeatedly was someone that my mother trusted, and she believed he had her back. That is the profile of most pedophiles. Our children need to be in healthy, well-rounded environments.

A healthy environment provides the necessary ingredients our children need to develop into the great people they were destined to be. God has great things in store for us; however, the devil's goal is to steal them, kill them, or ultimately destroy everything God has stored up for us. We must learn how to combat the devil and get back what was stolen from us. We also need to teach our children how to submit themselves to the Lord, and the devil will flee from them. What I mean is, we must start to tell our children the truth about life and what goes on in life. We must stop assuming they are too young to talk to about certain things.

When we as a parent fail to talk to our children and explain the right way and tell them why it is imperative to listen and be obedient, that's when we open up the door for the streets to talk to them and train them. I know this sounds impossible, but it will be if we don't do anything. We must save our children and provide great examples (even if we are parenting as a single parent). Ask your children questions but provide a comfortable and conducive environment for them to trust you with their conversation. That is very important in a relationship between children and their parents. So much stuff happens in the course of the day with us parents, can you imagine what your children must go through?

If we start talking to them when they can speak, the conversation won't be hard later. Parents, talk to your sons and daughters. Make them comfortable to talk to you about anything and everything. However, you must set boundaries because they are your children and not your friend. We are raising great sons and daughters. God has entrusted us with the greatest assignment in the world, raising His children. Always remember we have to give an account to God for the job we've done. So let's do the best job ever!

What The Devil Meant For Bad

When a woman is pregnant with a child, that is supposed to be one of the happiest times in her life. Bringing new life into the world is a sign that God is still doing great things. But sometimes, we can make things complicated with the decisions that we make. I am a child born out of a secret affair. It was secret because my father was married and had a family. I was conceived out of an unhealthy situation.

Miz Melanie's Moments:
We must think about the decisions that we make. My parents did not plan my conception. However, God knew about my arrival. My parents were messing around, and my mother got pregnant. The Bible says in Numbers 32:23 that our sin will find us out. My father knew that he had a wife and children at home, but he still decided to mess around with my mother. I do not believe that he would have messed around with my mother if he knew that a child would be conceived from his actions. My parents decided without thinking about the ramifications of their actions. These kinds of decisions are made every day. Children are born in these kinds of situations, which leads to single parenting, broken homes, and our children being broken due to these decisions.

This is the first problem I encountered as a newborn baby entering the world. This is a situation that a lot of children face at the beginning of their lives. Shortly after I was born is when I encountered abandonment and rejection. As a child, the devil had already set a trap for my life in plain sight, and nobody recognized his moves. That's how the devil works. He gets a foothold into your space when you're not looking, and he sits there until he can make a bigger impact. He's quiet, cunning, and strategic about his work because his purpose is to ruin your life and keep you from your destiny and the great things God has stored up for you.

Miz Melanie's Moments:
Life is like a maze with a lot of paths. You have to decide which path you want to take. As a parent, you are the authority for your children. Parents make the initial decisions for their children, and those decisions determine which paths and directions your children will take in life. And that's exactly what he did in my life.

He came after me as a baby, and he started with eliminating my father from my life.

Miz Melanie's Moments:
The first man that a girl falls in love with is her father. If her father is absent, it leaves a void in her heart and her life. Suppose her father has abandoned and rejected her from the beginning of her life; that sets a pattern for her life unless that

cycle is broken. How are other men that she meets after the rejection and abandonment of her father supposed to treat her? A girl looks for the same kind of love she received from the beginning of her life. A boy whose father is absent automatically assumes the father of the house role. He tries to fill in for the absent father, and he has to figure the role out according to the needs of his single mother.

I grew up the first part of my life estranged from my father because he was married. That meant the nurturing and reassuring love that I needed from my father I didn't get. Due to the circumstances that I was conceived and born into, I was deprived of that important relationship.

Miz Melanie's Moments:
This is something that should be taken into consideration before a child is conceived. A child, a new life is a responsibility, a shared responsibility. It's an assignment from God. Always remember that you will have to give an account to God at the end of your days for your child's life. So fathers don't allow the mother of your child to keep you from your child's life. However, mothers have to allow the fathers to be fathers to their children.

My father was not present in his role because of his circumstances. It was an accident and a secret due to the decisions my father and mother made.

Miz Melanie's Moments:
Both parents are very important to the development of a child. Each parent has a significant role in the development of a child's life. As children (especially girls), we need balance, and that's what both parents are supposed to provide for their children. Fathers are a unique part of that balance. For girls, their father is the first man in their lives. They are the first man they love, their protector, their provider, and the man who sets the role for every man she will meet from that day forward. Fathers give their daughters the gift of self-confidence and high self-esteem. Daughters that are given these tools from their fathers grow up to be happy and successful adults. When that man (father) is absent, there is a void left in the daughter's life. That void she tries to fill with her first boyfriend. Father's right here is when your daughters need you to be present in their lives. This is the time when the boyfriend's words are the most effective.

My mother told me another man was my father due to my father being married.

Miz Melanie's Moments:
Right here is where turmoil enters the picture. How do we expect children to process this? This is a lie, and then we teach our children not to lie to us. That lie made things much more complicated. Remember, we lie to hide and cover-up something (the truth).

My father also had children that did not know he had fathered a child outside of his marriage. I grew up thinking my father was a family friend that favored me. He would come over on some Saturdays, and my mother would always call me in the house to see him. He would ask me questions about how I was doing. He would tell me to be a good girl and listen to my mother. He would say things like, I better not get a bad report on you. I would pay close attention to every word he said. He was a smooth, handsome guy with a lot of charisma and soft spokenness. He was very interested in how I was treated, which felt weird to me because he was supposedly a family friend. Being a child, I never really put much thought into it.

I actually called him (my father) "Mister" before knowing he was my father. My mother taught respect in our home. I was always respectful, and I always used my manners. However, he (my father) did have a special love for me, and I could sense that as a child. Also, he would always give me twenty dollars. When I was a child, that was a lot of money, making me feel special. I loved when he came around. Little did I know, he was my father. I grew up very active. I was seemingly a happy child. I loved to play outside with my friends. I loved to play alone when I had to stay in the house. I have always had a bubbly personality, and I always wanted everyone to be happy. I was always trying to have fun, laugh, and I wanted to convey that energy to everybody I came in contact with.

As a child, I had a mischevious side too. I would find things to get into, maybe because no one was paying attention to me. As for my mother, being a single parent in the '60s was not an easy task. She was often challenged with the cares of life and the absence of my father. However, I had a stepfather that was in the house for a few years. One day my stepfather and my mother were in a huge fight. My mother told him to get out, he left and never came back home to live. I could never understand what happened. To this day, I still don't know what happened.

Every time my mom would tell him to get out before that time, she would tell me to get out too. That was devastating to me as a child. He would get in his car and drive away, and I would be left sitting on the steps crying until my mother would let me come back into the house. My mother would say to me, "since you like him so much, you get out with him." This was her husband, my stepfather, a man she brought into my life. How could she say those things to me? I was a child six and seven years old.

Miz Melanie's Moments:
Parents, we probably don't realize in those moments of anger that we traumatize our children. In this situation, I was traumatized by the fight and the fact that I was put out of the house. As a child, I was left to try and process those feelings alone. I realized later on in life that I compartmentalized those feelings. Those feelings showed up later in

different situations in my life. I was just an innocent child and a casualty of their war.

My mother was also a disciplinarian. When my mother spoke, you listened and did what you were told, or you would face major consequences. There were rarely any second chances. My mother seemed to be frustrated a lot of the time because of the decisions she made. Sometimes that meant I had to feel the wrath of her frustration. That's when I experienced the first signs of abuse. I experienced physical, mental, and verbal abuse. If the laws that exist for child abuse today were in place when I was growing up, my mother would have been jailed for her version of chastisement. My mother would yell at me when she was angry and called me all kinds of derogatory names. I was called "bitch" or "dumb ass" regularly. I remember from as far back as three years old hearing my mother call me bad. She would tell me that I was "so damn bad." She would say, "you get on my damn nerves with your badass self."

Miz Melanie's Moments:
One of the things I learned about raising children is not to chastise your children when you are angry. You say and do things in those moments that you can not take back, and you will live to regret it. Especially if you leave these things unfinished, those things you did not like done to you as a child, don't repeat the same behavior. Sometimes parents repeat the same behavior without even realizing they are doing it. Address your wrongs, your

shortcomings, your mistakes, and then talk about them with your children. When you face it, you can fix it. Also, please don't call your children names; it hurts. Those things you call your children in anger follow them throughout their life.

Children form into the things you call them. If you call your child smart and tell them they will be even smarter if they read 100 books, that child will read 100 books to be smarter. Children are easily influenced and especially by their parents. Positively speak to your children and make a great impact on their lives. The difference in my home is that my children would tell me that I hurt them. We talked about what they were feeling, and it allowed me to see things from their view. This is very important to your children. You are letting them know that their feelings are important to you, and you are concerned about their feelings. Let your children know that their feelings matter. And in doing so, you must keep boundaries. Children are smart, and they know how to seize (milk) the moment. It's a challenging assignment to raise a child. God has given you an important assignment raising His children. We all belong to God; we are all His children. At the end of the assignment, we have to give an account of what we did with the assignment. This is not an easy task, especially when you are doing the job alone. However, you can do it!

My self-esteem was destroyed, and I felt worthless as a child. I have full lips (that I have now grown into, and women get botox to have lips like mine today), and I was teased because of them. My mother would even tease me about my lips, which made things worse for me. It's one thing to have the kids in the neighborhood teasing me, but it's even worse when it comes from your parents. My mom would call me when she was drinking her coffee and ask me to cool her coffee off with my big lips. She would refer to my lips as coffee coolers. That was humiliating, belittling, degrading and hurtful. And it was coming from my mother. I had no self-confidence as a child. I never was made to feel beautiful; I always felt very ugly. How awful is that to say to a child. And then my mother would laugh. How humiliating. I would laugh too because laughing made me feel accepted, and it was a happy moment at home. That was really degrading, and it made me feel horrible inside.

Miz Melanie's Moments:

Parents don't belittle or disgrace your children. That's one of the worst things you can do to your child. That's called killing them with your tongue. Imagine how that must feel to have to endure that at home and then go to school, and the kids badger you too. It was awful, and I was expected to achieve in school while carrying the weight of several types of abuse. That's mental and emotional abuse, and it kills a child's s self-esteem and self-confidence. These kinds of statements come from a place of hurt inside of you. This is how we cause our children to have mental health issues.

My mother had a lot of pain that she compartmentalized, and it came out on her children.

Miz Melanie's Moments:
Most times, these things derive from the hurt you are feeling from the absences of your father or the pain of that relationship. That same behavior I inflicted on my children without even knowing it. I was repeating a behavior that I despised without even realizing it. I would say, " you are acting just like your father " to my children. I was saying these things from the space that I did not like in their fathers. I was not saying these words from a place of love, joy, or greatness. These words were meant in a derogatory way, in anger, bitterness, and sometimes hate. This is emotional and mental pain that I inflicted on my children without even knowing it. My children would check me in the heat of the situation. "Mom, please don't say that to me; I am not my father." Then we would discuss and unpack what happened and how that made them feel. My daughters would tell me to stay on topic. If I am chastising them about something, stay on topic, the other stuff is hurtful.

I grew up believing I was ugly and worth nothing. I would try to do whatever I could to keep things joyful in our home. I hated when my mother was angry, and our household was hostile. I learned at an early age to suppress and hide my feelings. I came up in an era where you did not talk back to adults. My mother never shared her business with me. In that era, the parents were the adults, and the children were children. I did not speak unless adults spoke to me. I was taught to stay in a child's place, which meant do not talk in adult conversations. When adults are talking, I would never interject my opinions, thoughts or say a word unless asked a question.

Miz Melanie's Moments:
Today, children talk, interrupt, and add their opinions in adult conversations, which bothers me. Nothing seems to be off-limits with the children today. There should be boundaries between you and your children. If no boundaries are created, you leave the door open for your children to be rude and disrespectful.

As a child, when I would get beaten, sometimes the kids in my neighborhood could hear me screaming. They would tease me because I would be screaming so loud. After all, they could hear what was going on. I would be so embarrassed. At times my mother would beat me with an extension cord. After a while, I was no longer embarrassed because it was a part of my life. This is heartbreaking because I had normalized the abuse. I had learned to accept emotional, mental, and physical abuse as love. When kids from my neighborhood would get mad at me, they would say, I am going to tell your mother, and she is going to beat your butt. That is how normalized it was.

I remember lashing out in anger as a child with my friends when things did not have the outcome I wanted. I would always want to fight everybody because that was my defense mechanism. That was bottled-up anger from the abuse I was enduring as a child.

Miz Melanie's Moments:
As parents, you probably don't realize abuse in all forms has a major effect on your children and their mental health. Abuse can cause underachievement in our children. Also, when we have a bitter breakup, it affects the children. It can make them fearful of expressing how they feel about the breakup. It makes things awkward for them, and they don't know how to express that they want to see the other parent. If you are constantly arguing and saying horrible things about the other parent, that could make the child afraid of saying they want to see the other parent. We can hurt our children severely by just what we say about the other parent. No matter how you feel about the other parent, that is still their parent. Also, if the other parent, especially fathers, doesn't come and spend time with the child because they don't like the mother, that damages a child sometimes to no repair. Mothers, please don't keep your children away from their fathers because you are hurt that things didn't work out with you and their father. Fathers, if you and the mother of your children don't work out, please come and see your children. It is important

to your child that they see you and spend time with you. When you and the mother of your child do not work out, it leaves a lot of unanswered questions for your child that they don't know how to ask. It's a difficult situation for your child to try and verbalize. That's all I will say about that right now!

Daddy Issues

When I was ten years old, I was very popular in my neighborhood. I was happiest when I played with my friends and rode my bike with the other kids in the neighborhood. I remember coming back from Detroit, Michigan, on vacation. All of my friends were so happy to see me; I felt like a celebrity. All the kids in the neighborhood were crowding around me and asking me questions about my plane ride and my trip. Most of the kids in my neighborhood had never been on an airplane before. A lot of the things I told them I made up because the real reason I had gone to Detroit, Michigan, was to see a man I was told was my real father.

As it turns out, he was my so-called godfather because my real father was married. I had to stay with his brother, his brother's wife, and their children. My uncle and his wife were nice, but I didn't feel like they wanted to be burdened with caring for me full-time while in Detroit. I really didn't get to see my so-called father/godfather a lot, which was strange because that was the initial reason for my visit. I saw him a few times throughout the visit. I wanted to spend more time with him because I didn't see him often due to him living out of town. I just heard a lot of stories about him.

When I came back home from my vacation, my mom seemed so different; some things had changed in my home. My mother had moved someone into our house. The new person was a man, and his name was Mr. Raymond. He seemed like a nice and friendly man. My mother told me he would be living with us for a while, and he was renting my bedroom. I was sad because I did not like that this man was now living in my room.

As a child, I would not dare open my mouth to say what I did not like because my opinion did not matter. I was a child, and I was told to stay in a child's place. If I had an opinion about Mr. Raymond renting my room, I had to keep that to myself. Plus, I did not pay any bills. My mother was not the parent you would talk back to or even say you disliked a decision she made. She was head of our household, and she made the decisions. My mother would slap me upside my head and say, "That's for what you are thinking."

The plan was for him to live in our home until he got married. I later found out from listening to my mother talking on the phone that she moved Mr. Raymond into our house because she needed that extra money. My stepfather's income was no longer coming in, so renting my room helped my mother with her bills. Mr. Raymond would pay his rent on time and sometimes give my mother extra money.

All of my aunts and uncles seemed to like this man as well. It seemed as if they made him an honorary uncle. Mr. Raymond was barely there a lot overnight, so I did not understand why he had to rent my room. He would only come there to bring his girlfriend {not the woman he was getting married to} and other women to have sex with. If I was in the house when he would be in the room with those women, I would leave.

They were very loud, and if my mother came in and thought I was listening to what adults were doing, I would be in big trouble. He would come to the house in the afternoon from work and be in the room for a few hours with his women. My mother was a hard-working single parent. She worked full time, went to school part-time in the evenings a few nights a week, sold dinners, sold alcohol, ran numbers, and she held card games in our home on the weekends. This was how she was able to pay her mortgage, her bills and give her children the best of everything.

My mother did not want us to suffer in life; she did the best she could with what she had and what she knew. My mother showed her love by giving me things. She gave us the best, and she wanted the best for us. She was not a hugger; she did not say, "I love you," and she showed little to no affection. But she loved us. Every person that came to my house knew that my mother did not allow any adults, especially men, to talk to her children.

My mother was tough, and she made that clear. A child should stay in a child's place, and a child should be seen and not heard. She made people respect her, her children, and her house. My mother never allowed her children to participate in conversations with adults. If my mother thought I was looking or listening to an adult talking, I would get slapped right in the mouth. That is how strongly she felt about children staying in their place.

Every weekend around the time for things to get started, my mother made sure we had eaten our dinner, taken our baths, in our pajamas, and up in our room. Mr. Raymond was always there on the weekends, and he would pick up certain things, like cases of beer and alcoholic beverages, for my mother's weekend events. He was very helpful and always offered to do things to help out and take some of the pressure off my mother. I think that was one of the reasons why my mother trusted him.

He was a very sexual and a very playful man with the ladies. Mr. Raymond was a heavy drinker; he was always feeling all over the women's bodies who came over to visit my mother. He would say very nasty and perverted things to them, and they would just laugh. I could not understand why everybody would laugh at the derogatory, belittling, and degrading things he would say to women. The women seemed to like it, and they would laugh along with everyone else.

I Always Loved The Lord

When we moved to our new home, there were still a lot of white families living in the neighborhood. My next-door neighbors were white. One day my next-door neighbor's daughter invited me to church. I started going to church with my new friends Theresa and Lidia every Sunday. I attended the Episcopal church a few blocks away from my house. I loved that church.

My pastor was Rev. Mulch, and he was the nicest man I had ever met. I was happiest when I went to church. It was the late sixties early seventies. It still baffles me when I look back on those times. I never knew the racial tension the country was going through at the time because no one treated me differently. Everybody was the same in my church. It was like the church didn't see race, and I was never made to feel inadequate, unequal, or unwanted.

I had my Holy Confirmation service, where I was confirmed (saved) at age nine. I had to wear all white which to me represented my life being cleansed. I felt like a bride because I also had to wear a veil. That day was so special to me, and I will remember that day forever. My mother, my godmother, my godfather, and family and friends attended the service. It was really a big day for me, and I felt like I was a princess. I was in the choir, went to Sunday school and Bible study. It seemed like every time the doors of the church were opened; I was there. After a while, Theresa and Lidia weren't going to church as much as I was going. In the summer, they would go down the shore, but it didn't stop me. I met new friends at church, and I enjoyed being there. The pastor, Rev. Mulch had the voice of an angel. When he would do the Holy Communion services, his voice rang throughout the church. He would say as he gave the bread and wine, "This is the body and blood of our Lord and Savior Jesus Christ preserved for our body and soul, take and eat in remembrance of Him."

Then he served the bread and then the wine. He gave the entire congregation the wine out of the communion cup. We all drank from the same cup, and he would wipe the cup with the napkin and then serve the next person on the altar. It was real wine, and it would burn my chest. It always seemed like I would get a big sip every time. After taking the communion, I always felt and knew that something great and powerful had happened to me. I did not know how to verbalize it, but I just knew. When I gave my life to the Lord, it was at an Episcopal Church. I started as an Episcopalian and have been steadfast ever since.

Molested as a Child

M r. Raymond was seemingly helpful to my mother, always offering to do things to help her. It appeared he was making life a little easier, but it was really a setup. He would tell my mother not to worry about the house because he would be stopping over to check and make sure everything was all right. He was setting up to infiltrate his next victim, and that victim was me. He was a master manipulator, child abuser, and molester, just to name a few. It was sunny outside in the middle of the day, and Mr. Raymond called me. I was riding my bike back and forth up and down the driveway with my friends. I told my friends I would be right back; Mr. Raymond was calling me.

When I went into the house, I did not see him, so I said, "yes, Mr. Raymond," and he said, "come upstairs. I want you to go to the store for me". So I ran up the steps, and I stood in the hallway by the stairs waiting for him to give me the money and tell me what he wanted from the store. I just wanted to hurry up so I could get back outside. In those days, you could leave your bike outside overnight, and no one would touch your bike. Then Mr. Raymond asked me if I had ever let a boy touch my kitty cat, and he pointed to my vagina.

I answered very defensively, "no."

He said, "let me see," and I immediately started to cry and defend myself. At that moment, I felt like I was guilty of a crime at ten years old.

"I said I never let any boys touch my kitty cat."

Mr. Raymond said "I am going to check, and if I find out you let some boys touch you down there, I'm going to tell your mother, and you know what she will do to you if she finds out."

I was crying hysterically and scared to death. I knew that if my mother even thought that I had let some boy touch my vagina, I was going to get my butt beat badly. The kind of beating she would put on me, I would not be able to sit down for a few days. Today people go to jail for beating their children like that. I had never let a boy do anything to me; I was still a little girl.

Miz Melanie's Moments:

These are the traits and signs of a pedophile. They tend to be well-liked by your parents, family, and friends. In this case, Mr. Raymond was well-liked by my mother, family, and friends. Pedophiles seek out children who are quiet, needy, or have problems at home. They also find ways to be alone with your child. Many times pedophiles will develop a close relationship with a single parent in order to get close to their children. Once inside the home, they have many opportunities to manipulate the children—using guilt, fear, and love to confuse the child. If the child's parent works, it offers the pedophile the private time needed to abuse the child. My mother was not at home a lot due to work, school and a few nights, she worked as a bartender at the local neighborhood bar.

He told me to pull my pants and my panties down and lay across the bed. He already had his pants off, and he wrapped his penis in a towel. He started rubbing and fondling my vagina. He put his fingers in my vagina and was rubbing all over me. I can still remember his face with that smutty smile looking at me. I was lying there stiff, silently crying frantically. I felt like I had done what he had accused me of doing. That was the worst day of my life.

Then he started rubbing his penis really fast in a towel. All of a sudden, he let out this loud sound, and he ejaculated in the towel. He was moaning and groaning, and then he froze like a cartoon character. I was so scared I just wanted to get out of that room and leave. Mr. Raymond was acting like he was in space or something. He asked me if I liked what he had just done to me, and I said "no."

Then he said, "You will one day," and he laughed.

He told me to get up, fix my clothes, wash my face and go to the store for him. He told me he would not tell my mother about me this time, but if he finds out that I am allowing boys to touch me down there, he would tell her. He said he is going to keep checking to make sure I was telling the truth.

Miz Melanie's Moments:
If I had a relationship with my mother that I felt comfortable talking to her, I would have been able to tell her the first time Mr. Raymond touched me. This is how important having open communication with your children is. Because I did not have a relationship with my mother that I could come to her and tell her what Mr. Raymond had done to me, and I was afraid to approach her with this. He was able to continue to rape me for years.

After Mr. Raymond molested me, he sent me to the store with $5.00 to get him a soda, and when I came back with the soda, he said I could keep the $4.50 change. Any other time if someone had given me $4.50, I would have run to the store so fast. But this time, I was not excited about the money. I was devastated. I did not know what to do after that experience. For a little girl, ten years old, that was a lot to process. I remember my best friend Spankie asking me where I had been. I felt guilty and dirty. I thought he knew what had just happened to me, even though he was not there. I responded I was in the house. I had to do something. Spankie was two years older than me and very nosey. He was always spying on people and telling other people their business. He was older than me and very bossy. I could talk to Spankie about anything. A year later, I told Spankie that Mr. Raymond was molesting me, and he wanted to set him up to get caught.

I was really all for it, but then I felt like I would get in trouble for doing something like that. Spankie could get away with stuff like that at his house because his parents were separated, and he was the man of the house. When I told him about Mr. Raymond, he said "I always knew it was something strange about him."

He said he never trusted him with those dark sunglasses on all the time. Spankie was like my girlfriend; It was a rumor that Spankie was gay, but that was taboo when I was a child. You could never declare that in public. He had girlfriends, and he played with his boyfriends too. Besides, I did not care what people said about Spankie; he was my friend. That day after it happened, I stayed outside all day. I didn't even go into my house to use the bathroom.

Mr. Raymond left my house before it was time for my mother to come home. I was afraid to go into the house because I did not know if Mr. Raymond had told my mother that story he threatened to tell her. The story he made up about me letting boys touch my kitty cat. I saw my mother get off the bus and walk to the front door. My heart was beating fast. I tried to look in the other direction so we would not make eye contact.

Then Spankie said "Jackie," Jackie was my nickname, "Your mother is home from work."

I turned and looked, and my mother called me in the house. I was sure I was in big trouble. All sorts of thoughts were going through my head; I thought Mr. Raymond called my mother at work and told her that story; I thought she was going to beat me as soon as I walked through the door. I did not know what to expect as I approached the door.

Then my mother asked me the big question...did I do my chores. Oh, what a sigh of relief. I quickly answered, "yes, mom, I did."

She answered, "I better not find out that you rushed through your chores just to get outside to ride that bike."

I replied again, "Yes, mom."

My mother allowed me to go back outside and play. I was so relieved that I did not get in trouble that I went to the store and spent the money Mr. Raymond gave me with Spankie. If my mother found out that I had money and she did not give it to me, I would get in trouble for that too. I had to spend it all before I went into the house. I didn't know how to explain where the money came from. I was so glad that was over, and now I could try to resume being a little girl again. As I would soon find out, that would be hard to do.

Every time I would go to the bathroom, it would sting really badly, but I would not dare tell anyone. I started to believe I had allowed boys to play with my kitty cat. I was trapped in this illusion Mr. Raymond had made up, and I had no one to tell who would believe me. I was a kid, and he was an adult.

Miz Melanie's Moments:
Here is where there was a disconnect between my mother and me. I never felt like I could talk to her about anything. There was no environment to talk in my home. There should always be a space allowed for your children to talk. Children should be able to talk freely to their parents without being

judged or chastised. Talking with your children is always an opportunity to teach them. Parents should also listen to their children. You learn a lot about your child and how they feel if you just listen.

Every time Mr. Raymond would come over to my house, he would molest me. After he got away with it the first time, it started happening more and more. One morning I was home doing my chores while my mother was at work. I could not go outside until I finished cleaning the bathroom. I was cleaning the tub in the bathroom, and I did not know Mr. Raymond was in the house. I was home alone at the time, I heard someone coming up the steps, I came from the bathroom to look and see who was coming up the stairs and it was nasty ole Mr. Raymond.

He went into that middle room, and he called me into the room. He asked me if my mother called, I said "no." He asked me if I finished doing my chores, and I answered almost. He said good because he needed me to do something for him. Standing there like he was a concerned family friend. Always plotting how he was going to make his next move. He was a master manipulator, and he studied his prey. I was just a little girl naïve to his tricks. It makes me cry even now to think about how he would prey on my innocence. He gazed at me with a sick look, with those crossed eyes behind those tinted glasses. He called me into the room. When I went into the room, he was naked and immediately I started to cry.

He said, "lay across the bed. I am not going to hurt you. I just want to check you again to make sure you are not doing anything with those little boys I see you playing with. You know your mother would kill you if she ever found out you let all of those boys touch you down there."

One of his tricks was to interject fear in me, and then he would be able to rape me. I was afraid of my mother and what she would do to me. He was able to use that because he had observed my mother and how she ran her household. He could get to me because he posed as a friend who cared about her and her situation. He knew there wasn't a father in the home. He knew her schedule when she would be at work, the nights she was at school, and the nights she worked at the bar. He studied her, and he acted like a brother. A brother that was there to help his sister and her children. I had no idea what he was talking about. I played with boys and girls.

I laid across the bed so frightened and stiff. He started to rub all over my vagina, making sounds, rubbing his penis. Then he said, "you have been letting them boys touch you, I can tell."

I was crying hysterically, saying "no, I didn't, no, I didn't."

He said I need to check some more. Tell me if this hurts, and he tried to stuff his penis in my vagina, and I screamed. He put his hand over my mouth. He said "it won't hurt you, just let me put it in a little bit."

I kept crying hard. He said, "that let's me know boys have been touching you down there because it hurts when I touch you."

Then his penis fell between my legs, and he humped on me until he ejaculated on my thighs; all of this wet white sticky stuff was all over me. He was dazed and panting. For a few seconds, he laid there naked, almost like he forgot where he was. He was caught up in the moment. If my mother had come into the house, he would have been caught that day. He gave me some money and told me to get myself together and go back outside. He said that he would not tell my mother about me this time because I was being good.

I felt a sigh of relief again. I started to believe it was my fault that Mr. Raymond was doing this to me. I hated Mr. Raymond, and I hated my mother for letting him move into our house. I wanted my stepfather to come back home, but I hardly ever saw him anymore. I knew if my stepfather were living with us, none of this would be happening. I started to get to know his pattern, and if I saw him before he saw me, I would disappear. The problem was if he arrived at my house while I was still there, that was how he would be able to launch his attack.

One day, I was hanging up the laundry on the clothesline in the basement, and Mr. Raymond came into the house. He was so crafty and sneaky. Sometimes you didn't even know he was in the house. When I heard him calling to ask if anyone was home, I left out the back door. I remember getting in trouble because I did not finish hanging up the clothes, and they mildewed, but I didn't care. I had enough of him raping me whenever he felt like it. I was developing into a young girl. I had breasts, and this man would rape me at will.

Mr. Raymond got to the point where he did not use the lie that he was checking to see if the boys had touched me. He would just start kissing me in the mouth with his tongue forcefully and sucking my breast even though I would try to resist. It seemed like he liked the fact that I resisted him. He forced my pants down and pushed his huge penis in my vagina, and I screamed so loud that my nosey neighbor asked me what I was screaming for when I came outside.

One day he came over and tried his usual routine on me. I was washing dishes in the kitchen, and he came behind me, grinding on my butt like we were a couple. At that point, I lost it; I would no longer let this man take advantage of me anymore. I started cursing very loudly, and I took a butcher knife and started stabbing at him. I was crying, and I did not care if anyone came into the house or what anybody had to say.

I was no longer going to let him rape me again. I had reached my limit, and I was out of control. This was a dangerous moment in my life, and I thank God that I didn't stab him or even kill him at that moment. I was in a rage, and I had enough of him raping, tormenting, and sexually abusing me. I could not understand how a grown man could find pleasure in having sex with a child. That's when I started to hate my mother because how could she let this monster in our house? How did she not know what he was doing to me, and where was she? He had destroyed me from the inside out, physically and emotionally.

The trauma from childhood sexual abuse would have a lasting effect on my life for years to come. Mentally I was not able to move past the abuse for years. As a child, how could I comprehend or process what was happening to me? I was now a victim emotional, mental, physical, and sexual abuse, and I was still a child. If my mother had walked into the house that day, I would have just had to deal with the consequences.

Mr. Raymond started to laugh, and he was acting like I was funny. I was as serious as serious could get, and he was going to feel my anger that day. He tried to get the knife from me, but I kept swinging that knife. He managed to get the knife out of my hand. He was only able to pull my shirt up and suck on my breast. After wrestling with me, he said "I am going to leave you alone today, your period must be on."

Then he left, and I felt a sigh of relief. I was still very angry and still crying. I felt like I had no one in the world to talk to. I felt like no one in the world cared about me. I felt scared, alone, and like no one saw me. I began to talk to myself about how hurt I was and why I was so ugly that nobody cared for me. My stepfather was gone, my mother was working or going to school, and I was left with no one to watch over me. At twelve, there was a lot on my plate. I had been put in a predicament like a grown woman when I was a child. My body was changing, and I was no longer a virgin. I had been forced to do things grown-ups did, and I was still a child.

By the age of 12, so much happened in my life. My life changed drastically, and my mother or father did not know.

Miz Melanie's Moments:
It was easy for Mr. Raymond to sexually abuse me because he witnessed my mother's physical, mental, and emotional abuse. He was then able to manipulate me because he used the ammunition from my mother. He knew a man was not in the home, and he knew that I was not in contact with my father or my stepfather. Mr. Raymond also knew the relationship my mother, and I had. So this made it easy for him to attack me repeatedly. Parents, especially single parents, be careful who you allow to babysit or spend time alone with your children. Child sexual predators often make themselves available to help where there is a need. Creating an atmosphere of trust and dependency. Child sexual predators always make sure they build trust with the parent (especially single mothers). They created an environment to make the child feel like they can trust them too.

By the time I was ten years old, four men in my life had let me down. My Father, stepfather, godfather, and the man who raped me (Mr. Raymond). I was damaged goods at a time when children are supposed to be living a careless life of fun, joy, and happiness. Instead,

I was suffering a horrible trauma that would plague my life for over five decades.

Daddy, I Miss You

On one particular Saturday, my biological father (Mr. Fred) came over to visit. When he got there, my mother told me to take a bath and change my clothes because we were going out. I took my bath, got dressed, and we all got in Mr. Fred's car. At this point, I still don't know that Mr. Fred is my father. He always drove a nice up-to-date American-made car. We went to this restaurant with just the three of us for brunch. It was between lunch and dinnertime. The adults were talking, and they asked me what I wanted to eat. Things were going just fine, I loved Mr. Fred, but I felt bored.

Then the evening took a different turn. Mr. Fred started asking me questions about myself. As I was answering his questions, he told me that he and my mother dated before. My eyes got big because I just thought they were good friends. He told me they were in love and had a baby girl, and that baby girl was me. Then Mr. Fred hit me with a shocker.

He said, "I am your father."

I could have fallen out of my chair. I sat there quietly, and then tears started to roll down my face. He asked me why I was crying.

I answered, "I don't know, " but I was shocked to find out that Mr. Fred was now my father. Because kids did not have an opinion in that generation, I did not know what to say. It was not something I was asked often, so I was lost for words. He told me he wanted to wait until the right time to tell me.

He told me he loved me and always loved me from the first day he laid eyes on me. He told me that something happened between him and my mother that was none of my business, and that is why they waited until now to tell me. He asked me if I had any questions to ask him, and I said "no."

I was a child; what was I going to say? I was scared and didn't know what to say. The rest of the evening was weird because they flirted, laughed, drank, and talked about old times. Then Mr. Fred, I mean my father, drove us home, and he stayed the night. That night was perfect in so many ways for me. My parents were together in my home. It was a fantasy that I had as a child; to live in a house with both of my parents. A dream most children have. It only lasted for that night, but it brought me joy in a strange way.

The next day Big Momma came over after church. Big Momma was my grandmother, my mother's mother. I overheard my mother telling Big Momma that she and Mr. Fred told me he was my father. Big Momma did not hold back anything. She said whatever came to her mind and did not care if you did not like it. Big Momma spoke the truth and her mind. Big Momma said y'all should have been told that child Fred was her father.

My mother said, "Well, Big Momma, he was married at the time." Big Momma said he was married when you got pregnant, so what was the difference in telling her then or now. She said "That child should have known Fred was her father. I don't know how y'all was able to keep it a secret this long. The child looks just like him, look at her lips," and they both started to laugh.

I was upstairs and overheard the conversation. I immediately looked in the mirror to see what they saw. I wanted to see if I looked like him. I missed Mr. Fred already...oops, I mean, I missed my father already. I was so glad I was Mr. Fred's daughter because Mr. Fred was a nice guy. I spent the rest of the summer between my mother and my father's house. I did not know how to stop calling my father, "Mr. Fred." One day he said, "Don't call me Mr. Fred, I am your father, call me daddy."

I fell in love with my father that day. I always thought he was the best man ever. He talked softly, dressed well, and smiled all the time. I blended right in with my sisters and brothers. That was the best summer of my life. Then things changed, and I don't really know why. I just stopped going to my dad's house, and he stopped coming over.

Torn And Ruined

My world was so different from other children's worlds. I had endured physical, emotional, mental, and sexual abuse when other children rode their bikes, played games, and jumped rope. I started not to care about anything. I was rebellious and angry, and I started to hang out with some bad people. I had a way of masking and hiding my feelings. People did not know I was hurting severely and torn apart inside. I learned to hide my feelings and go on like everything was great in my life. I always had a smile on my face, no matter how I was feeling inside. But in reality, I was a wreck inside. I started living like things did not matter to me. I did not care about myself; how could I? Nobody else cared about me.

Miz Melanie's Moments:
Parents, this was a time when I changed, and my mother didn't notice. My mother was busy dealing with life circumstances and other things. Don't be so busy that you don't notice the changes in your child's life. That could be a costly mistake that some children and parents never recover from.

My mother would take my sibling and me out to dinner at different restaurants every month. She taught us about our culture, taught us etiquette, and wanted our lives to be better than her life was. My mother even sent me to charm school under the direction of the fabulous Vera Gunn at the famous Freedom Theatre in Philadelphia. We would talk about surface things. Our conversations were never deep ones. My mother did most of the talking. Because I wanted to laugh, I would talk about funny stuff.

Miz Melanie's Moments:
Having a conversation with your children is extremely important. It is especially important to the development of your child that you notice a change in their life. Always have a casual conversation with your children. It builds relationships and trust. If you notice that their behavior or attitude changes, that is an indication that things have changed somewhere in their life. That's an important time to have conversations with your child. Suppose we, as parents, keep an open conversation. In that case, it will not be hard to ask your children, "can we talk about" or "do you want to talk about something." Conversations with your children are healthy, important and they build relationships!

     I began to get really promiscuous with the boys. I started letting the boys grind on me with my pants down. I guess this was when my quest started looking for someone to love me. I wanted to feel wanted and liked. I wasn't pretty, so I had to allow them to grind on me with my pants down for the boys to like me. This was the only way boys showed me attention. I was trying at this age to fill a void left open by my father.

Mr. Raymond destroyed me more every time he raped me. He solidified that I was ugly, unloved and that nobody cared about me. He was almost able to destroy me completely at a young age. I was now allowing boys to do these things Mr. Raymond accused me of. I did not care about myself, and I had no self-worth. I would let the boys put their penis between my legs and grind on me until they would ejaculate. We believed we were really having sex. We were defiantly unlearned with the sex thing, and my knowledge came from the man that raped me.

Spankie and I started hanging out with this new boy in the neighborhood. We started hanging out at his house because he had a bar in his basement. We would go over to his house when his mother was not home and drink alcohol at his mother's bar. When Spankie would turn his head, I would spit out my drink. Drinking alcohol tasted nasty, but I wanted to be a part of the crowd and escape my reality. I just wanted to go somewhere where no one could find me. Going over to this friend's house was an escape from my world. So much was out of control in my life, and I was not yet a full teenager. I was living recklessly because of what was done to me. Emotionally, I was suffering severely, and no one in my home had a clue. I thank God that He gave me the capacity and ability to continue living.

Miz Melanie's Moments:
These are 911 signs, parents! These kinds of things cause young people to commit suicide. Things like Traumatic Stress - Isolation from family due to

abuse - feeling alone - feeling hopeless - feeling rejected. These are some symptoms to look out for in your children. If you see any of these signs, you need to take a closer look at your child's life.

Living Reckless

I remember going to see my uncle in a detention center for family day. I met a boy there named Chet (that was his nickname). Chet was from South Philly, and I heard South Philly guys were hip and had it going on. I had my own phone in my room, and I would be talking to him on the phone all times of the night. My family never had a clue that he even existed. I hooked my best friend up with his friend over the phone. She never saw what he looked like in person. We did not have cell phones where we could send pictures or Facetime someone. We just went by how you sound over the phone and what your conversation was about. Today it's called online dating. Chet asked me to come down to South Philly to see him and bring my friend to see his friend. My best friend (Michelle) was dating Chet's friend from their phone conversation.

One day, we decided to go down to South Philly and be with our boyfriends (the boyfriends we basically met over the phone). We were young, naïve girls from uptown, and these guys were from the streets. My mother had no idea I was going to see him or that he existed. Michelle's mother and sisters knew where we were going; her mom was more down-to-earth. Michelle's mom would let us smoke over her house, and I loved that freedom. My mother would have made me eat the cigarette if she caught me smoking. Actually, she did make me eat a cigarette one time when she thought I was smoking.

When we left to go down South Philly, no one was home in my house. I knew I had to be home by a certain time. If I came back from South Philly by a certain time, no one would even miss me. We rode the bus downtown, and both of our boyfriends met us at the bus stop. Michelle and Michael met for the first time. Michael was Chet's friend and Michelle's boyfriend. We went to an apartment that Chet told me was his sister's apartment. This apartment was on the third floor of this apartment building.

As we walked into the apartment, I felt a little afraid, but I didn't want to make it known. After all, I had met this guy in a detention center and barely knew him. Chet and I were on one sofa, and Michelle and Michael were on another sofa. We were young, so we were just kissing and grinding. I felt like he was about to take things to the next level, and I did not know how to say no or that I was afraid. I was happy he was calling me his girlfriend. I did not want to say "no" because he might not like me anymore, or he probably would not want to see me anymore. I was always making up for being ugly, and I never felt like I was worth anything. I would do whatever I needed to keep boys interested in me.

Miz Melanie's Moments:
Our children, especially our daughters, need to feel love from their parents. That's where the foundation is laid. When a secure foundation is laid out for our children, they will not look for it in the streets. You can come from a two-parent home and

not have a good foundation. This should start when our children are born. The first piece of that foundation is love, affection, and security.

In one of my and Chet's phone conversations, he asked me if I loved him, and I said "yes."

Miz Melanie's Moments:
When a young boy/young man asks you if you love them, they set up their next move to get you to agree to have sex with them. That's an old trick that we must inform our daughters not to fall for. Fathers, you are an equal part of your child's life. Your child or children need you to be present in their lives. Time is more important than money. Some fathers don't come around because they are not financially equipped to support their children. Mothers are sometimes in the same predicament, but they stick around and do what needs to be done. Time is what you need! They need daddy to be consistent in their lives! Being a father present in a child's life is more valuable than gold.

To me, love meant somebody was paying attention to me. I didn't care that it was short-term. I was just happy with someone pursuing me. The kissing turned into a passionate kiss, and he began to unzip my pants. I kind of resisted him, but I knew it was coming. Then the door busted open. My heart was beating really fast, my pants were open, and I jumped up. In comes about fifteen guys from age 15 – 21. My heart was beating so fast, and Michelle started crying immediately. I hurried up and zipped up my pants, and fixed my clothes. All I could think about is "we are going to get raped by all of these guys today."

I looked at Chet, and he changed right before my eyes. He had a demeanor like a devil. He acted as if he did not know me and that I was not with him. I thought to myself; he set us up to be raped. I looked out the window to see if I could climb out the window, but it was a three-story drop from this apartment building. I had to think of something fast. Tears were rolling down Michelle's face like rain. She was scared, and so was I. I asked Chet why were these guys here?

The one I guessed was the oldest said, "we are going to give y'all what y'all came down here for."

Michelle started to scream, and he said, "shut up, girl, ain't nobody going to hear you up here." I just knew all those guys were going to rape us both repeatedly and probably kill us. Then the oldest guy said that he would let us go because Michelle was crying, but we had to kiss him before we left. I was so relieved; how hard could it be to kiss him and get out of there. He told me I had to go first, and he grabbed me, and as he was grabbing me, he said, "you're going first since you are the tough one."

I was not the tough one. I was probably more scared than Michelle. He laid a kiss on me that was unbelievable. He stuck his tongue almost all the way down my throat and grinded on me so hard as if he was having intercourse with me. His penis was so big and hard you could see it through his pants. He held me with a strong, firm hold and pressed his body against mine so hard. When he got finished, he pushed me on the floor and told me to move out of his way.

Miz Melanie's Moments:
My actions had caused me to be abused again. This happened to me because of several different reasons. I felt like nobody cared about me, so I did not care about me either. I found myself in this predicament that could have resulted in me and my girlfriend getting gang-raped and killed. God stepped in and changed the devil's plans. Thank You, Jesus!

He was a real mean guy, and then he proceeded to do the same thing to Michelle. He did not kiss and grind on her as long as he did me. I guess that was because she was screaming and crying. The other guys in the room were looking at us, laughing and talking about how scared we were. Then he opened the door and said, "get the fuck out of here before we pull a train on y'all stupid bitches."

I was so relieved and glad at the same time. We both ran all the way down those steps and all the way to the bus stop. When I got to the bus stop, I started laughing, and Michelle was so annoyed with me. She did not think anything was funny. I would always try to find humor in things, so I laughed as I talked about how our faces looked when those guys busted in the room. However, nothing was really funny. That incident could have ended horribly. We could have been raped, assaulted, and even murdered.

I thank God he had his hands on us even in our stupidity. We did not know their minds, and if I had to identify them, I couldn't. I didn't even know my boyfriend's real name. He told me his street name, which was Chet, and his friend's name was Michael. We were so young and naïve. These are the kinds of things young kids get themselves into when you do things without permission. None of my family members knew where I was or who I was with. Michelle's family knew we had gone down South Philly, but they did not know exactly where we were going.

Michelle was so mad and annoyed with me. She said, "Nothing is funny; Jackie, I will never go anywhere else with you again."

I was not mad, and I really didn't think what happened was funny. However, I was really glad we were out of there and on our way home. After that incident, I never spoke with Chet ever again. I am so glad that the incident had a somewhat happy ending.

Swim Like a Fish

I am now in junior high school, and I am starting the eighth grade. I am so excited for this year because I made the swim team. I never really participated in any after-school activities before. I was really excited because Coach Wally had chosen me for the team. I had a whole set of new friends that I would not have probably ever associated with if not for the swim team. We swam against other schools, and some of the schools were very competitive. Coach Wally believed in practice, so we practiced almost every day after school, especially before a swim meet. I had a little speed and upper body strength, so I swam the third leg of the freestyle. Coach told me he needed me to either keep us in the lead or catch us up when we were behind.

I knew I was a very important part of the team. I love to swim, but I hate getting my hair wet every day. If my hair was straightened, it would tighten up, and I would put it in a nappy ponytail. That ponytail looked a mess because my hair was not long. So, I would have a short nappy ponytail combed to the back or the top of my head. My friends were always making corny jokes about me being on the team because they were not on any activities in school.

I hung around the crowd that joked all the time, the kids the teacher would get so annoyed with them for interrupting class, being silly, and talking back. Those were the kids that played too much and had to stay after school for detentions for acting up trying to get attention. I was taking a risk hanging with this group because my mom permitted the disciplinarian teacher to beat my butt if I was disruptive.

Miz Melanie's Moments:
My mom was a single parent, and she could not take off her job to run back and forth to the school. So my mother permitted Miss Wnyder to chastise me when I was acting out in school. Miss Wnyder had the same temperament as my mother. Sometimes Miss Wydner would come down the hall and see me talking and knock me upside my head and tell me to get to class. Miss Wydner also talked with me, teaching me the importance of learning and what doors could be opened if I separated myself from the wrong crowd. Miss Wydner told me she would do everything she could to make sure that I made good choices, good grades, and found the right group to associate with. Miss Wydner was hard, but she had my best interest at heart. Miss Wydner understood that my mom was a single parent and trying to juggle a lot of things to make life better for me. I now thank God for Miss Wydner because she took the time to encourage me, and she was concerned about me. I am thankful for her input in my life because she did not have to, which was not in her job description. I was a little black girl going down the wrong path in school, and she sent me a life raft to steer me in the right direction.

I loved the swim team because I could be seen in a different view. The kids I hung with on the swim team had drive and ambition. Those kids were swimming for years and had hopes of going to college off of a swimming scholarship. They wanted to be something in life, and so did I. Being on the swim team made me feel important. I needed a new environment because I was involved in a big fight a few months before becoming a part of the swim team.

My sister fought this girl because she and her sister snitched on us for having company when my mother was not at home. My mother told us specifically not to have any company this particular night. The girl my sister was fighting was good friends with us, but I felt betrayed because they told my mother that we had some boys over our house. We had planned for all of us to entertain these guys that night. The girls asked their mother if they could come over, and their mother told them that they could not come over.

So, because my sister and I were defiant, my mother beat us unmercifully for disobeying what she told us to do. She told us not to have anybody in her house when she was not home, and we did anyway. So because the girls could not come over, they told on us, and we got in big trouble. My sister saw them walking in front of our house, and she went outside and confronted the oldest girl, and my sister started to fight her. Then both girls jumped my sister. I came outside to help my sister, and we ended up in a huge fight. The fight would continue for the next few days. The fight started up again in school. Someone told the girl that I was fighting that I was going to fight her after school. That was not true, but the person who spread that rumor was an instigator. I had detention after school that day.

Miss Wydner kept me after school for an additional hour that day because I was caught in the hallway. When I left school, I was by myself, and as I was walking home, I saw a big crowd waiting for me to get out of school. Obviously, there was an instigator who orchestrated this event. The girl that I was fighting was not a real fighter. She stayed out of school for a few days after the fight to avoid me. So, I was very surprised to see her waiting for me in the crowd.

Miz Melanie's Moments:
Parents teach your children to be their own person and have their own mind and voice. It's very important because instigators are dangerous people. They are not your friend. They start things and leave you out there all by yourself to handle what they started. An instigator is a trouble maker, and that makes them dangerous. This instigator who set this fight up convinced the girl I was fighting to stick around until I got out of school. She was able to keep the crowd waiting as well. I could have gotten killed that day because of an instigator. As I approached the crowd, I dropped my books and took off my jacket because I, too, had a reputation for fighting. The girl waiting to fight me was encouraged to stay there and fight me by the instigator.

The girl probably stayed and was not scared because she had a weapon. We started to fight, and I was getting the best of her, but little did I know she was really getting the best of me because she had a razor. I was fighting her with my hands, and she was cutting me with a razor. The school police drove up, and the crowd dispersed. He grabbed me because he knew I knew what was going on in the school. I was very popular in school. When he grabbed me, he said who was fighting, and then he discovered it was me. At that point, I discovered the girl had cut me, and I was bleeding profusely. She cut me with a razor 1/8 inch from my jugular vein and cut me behind my ear. My shirt was cut in the front, and blood was everywhere. I didn't even know I was cut. I could have died that day participating in a fight that I did not start.

The school police took me to the hospital, and at that time, the hospital could not work on me until a parent gave permission. I had to wait until someone could contact my mother. In the meantime, my uncle came to the hospital, and they would not allow him to give his consent because he was not my parent. I could have died that day. God always had his hands on me.

Miz Melanie's Moments:
The jugular vein is a major blood vessel that drains blood from your brain to every major organ in your body. If the jugular vein is cut, you can bleed to death within 5-15 seconds. That could have ended with me being dead and this girl going to jail for murder. We have to be very careful of the decisions that we make. Every decision that we make affects our future. For example: When one of my daughters

started to drive, she was a little heavy on the pedal. I told her to slow down when she drives. Don't be in a hurry to get to your destination. Then I explained to her that if she is driving and hits someone and they are killed, her life would change forever at that moment. So be careful of the decisions that you make every day of your life.

For me, the swim team was a new lease on life. It was a change of atmosphere and scenery. My teachers started treating me differently now because I was on the swim team. To be on the swim team, I had to keep good grades, and I could not be a discipline problem. I was determined to change the way my teachers and my friends perceived me. I even won a few trophies at the sports banquet. My school year had finally turned around for the better. When my swim practices were over, I would catch the bus home.

We moved after the big fight because my mother pressed charges against the girl. Me, my mother and the girl and her mother were going back and forth to court. My mother wanted the girl to go to jail, but the judge reprimanded both families and told the parents they need to teach us to live better lives. The judge was a black lady. She was angry to see two black families in her courtroom fighting over foolishness. She said that I could have died, and the girl I was fighting could have gone to prison for murder, and it didn't have to happen.

Because we moved, I now had to take the bus to school. I would ride the bus with this guy named, Little Reg. He was not popular like I was, and none of my friends knew him in school. Both of us would ride the bus to Germantown together every day after school. He would always wait for me to ride the bus with him. However, I had no idea he was waiting for me. When I would come out of school, he would already be at the bus stop. We would talk and hang out on the avenue before I would catch my next bus. I later found out that he liked me and that's why he would be waiting for me. I started liking him too because this was different for me. I acted as if I didn't like him around my friends because he wasn't popular as I was, and he was shorter than I was. I would joke around with him in school, but after my swim meets, we would always meet at the bus stop. We would go to the park and sit and talk for at least two hours.

We Got Something In Common

Lil Reg was a really nice and funny guy. We had a lot in common; he had a lot of problems and issues, just like me. We became very close because we both had family problems, and we both felt like the black sheep of our family. He would always have lots of money and weed. He introduced me to smoking weed, and I loved it. It seemed to take me away from reality. I needed to escape this world every chance I got.

Then one day, he asked me to go over to his grandmother's house. We started kissing and messing around. We were always on a time constraint because his aunt would come home from work at a certain time. I secretly lived for these after-school hook-ups so I could get high and indulge in these make-out sessions. My life was jacked up, and I could not tell anyone who would understand. Outside of everything, I always felt responsible for being sexually abused. I could talk to Lil Reg about being sexually abused, and he would always tell me it was not my fault. He told me not to feel guilty about what that creep did to me.

Little Reg would drink his uncle's whiskey due to his problems, and he would get drunk. Sometimes he would be so drunk I would leave him in the bed naked because I could not wake him up, and I did not want to get caught in the house when his aunt came home from work. We would have unprotected sex, and I had no clue I could get pregnant. Boy, was I dumb. There was no one to talk to about sex except my health teacher, and she taught very basic health education. At that time, sex was not often discussed, and sex was not the topic on every child's mind.

Pregnant At 14

We had sex every day for about four weeks straight after school. The next month went by, and I noticed my menstrual cycle did not come on, but I didn't pay attention because I did not keep a schedule. I would know my menstrual cycle was coming on by cramps or going to the bathroom and seeing a little blood in my panties. I believed I was too young to get pregnant. However, I knew I was pregnant at that moment. I don't know how I knew I was pregnant, but I just knew.

I wanted to believe that maybe I was just off that month, but deep down inside, I knew. Then it happened another month and another month. I knew I was pregnant for sure. I remember sitting on the toilet praying to God, begging Him to make my menstrual cycle come on. It seemed like God never heard that prayer. I was so scared I knew my life was over. I did not know what to do or expect when my mother found out. My breasts started to grow, and they were humongous, and my butt got bigger. I remember one of my uncle's asking my mother what she was feeding me because I was getting big. They laughed hysterically because, of course, he was making fun of me again. My jeans were so tight, and I didn't even plan that. The entire summer, I stayed in the house with my stepfather's old big pajamas on.

I only got dressed when I absolutely had to. No one in my family suspected anything because my mom and my sister were rarely home. And when my mother did notice I had on my stepfather's pajamas, she thought I had them on because I missed him. I finally told Little Reg that I was pregnant, and he seemed unbothered. He was probably high, and then one day, he called me and asked me if I was really pregnant? I said "Yes, I am pregnant, and this is not a joke."

He thought it was funny because he was laughing. He said "Everybody is going to know we were having sex now."

I was so angry with him because I knew I was in a lot of trouble. A baby is a lifelong commitment, and I never thought that far ahead. I was still dealing with how I was going to tell my mother that I was pregnant. I stopped talking to Lil Reg, and I stopped receiving his calls. At this point, I was trying to distance myself from him. I don't know what I thought that would do, but I needed some time to think. Days and days and more days went by, and I was growing bigger and bigger. I didn't know what to do, and I had no one to talk to.

Going Away For The Weekend

My sister and I planned to go to my aunt Rachel's house to see my cousin Bryan for the weekend. My cousin took my sister and me to a party, and I really wanted to go to this party. We had moved out of the neighborhood a few years prior, and I wanted to come back to hang out with my cousins. I was so excited to be going to this party because I was pregnant and needed an outlet.

My cousin was always in my business, and he acted more like a girl cousin than a boy cousin. So he asked me if I was pregnant because my breast was so big. I almost passed out. I said "No, I am not pregnant."

He was an expert with these kinds of things because he was the one that told me that my cousin Dana was pregnant at age 13. Dana and I were the same age.

He said, "You can fool your mother and sister, but you can't fool me. I know that you are pregnant, and the truth is going to come out soon."

I was nervous because I did not know who he would tell that I was pregnant. I had no idea. My aunt, which was my cousin's mother, was in the next room listening. We went to the party, and the party was jumping. They were smoking weed there, and the smoke was thick. I got a high contact, and I was feeling loopy and sleepy at the same time. My sister was there, and she had no idea I smoked weed, so I could not be caught smoking at this party.

I stood on the wall and watched as my cousin Bryan told my sister that I was pregnant. I saw the words come out of his mouth. My life was clearly about to change, and I did not know if it would change for the best or the worst. At that point, my sister came over to me with this big kool-aid smile saying, "are you pregnant?"

I thought I would die right there. My sister was jumping for joy. She was so happy. I don't know if it was the weed or if she was truly happy for me. My sister never knew how to keep a secret, and she was surely going to tell my mother. I am extremely nervous now. That night we went back to my cousin's house, and we stayed up all night talking about me being pregnant, and little did I know my aunt was in the other room listening to every word. Every closed eye ain't sleep.

The next morning my aunt called me into her room and asked me if I was pregnant. I was shocked. How did she know I was pregnant? Now my heart is beating over time, and I am scared to death. She said, "Pull up your nightgown and let me see your stomach." I pulled up my nightgown and held my stomach in as tight as I could.

My aunt said, "stop holding your stomach in. I know you are pregnant. I heard the entire conversation."

I started to cry, and she said there's no reason to cry now. Then she asked me if I told my mother that I was pregnant, and I answered no.

She then said, "Well, save those tears for your mother."

My mind is racing now because I don't know if she is about to call my mother and tell her that I am pregnant. Our weekend is over, and now I have to go home and face the music. I was so sure my aunt told my mother. When I got home, my mother was in an unusually good mood. I knew she didn't have a clue. A few days passed, and then the day had come, the moment of truth. My big-mouth sister told my mother I was pregnant.

My mother came in from work, and my sister said to my mother, "You are going to be a grandmother, and it's not me."

Well, who else could it be if my mother only had two children, two daughters, and it was not her? It had to be me. I was in my room, and I heard every word like they were on a microphone. I hated my sister at that moment. How could she be so evil and thoughtless? Why would she tell my mother something I should have told my mother? She was always trying to be better than me, she was always telling on me, and I hated that. Why couldn't she be a better sister and just talk to me? She had to know I was scared and afraid. I needed my sister to cover me and help me navigate a plan to tell my mother. But noooooo, my sister told my mother for me as usual, a tattle-tail. My sister always told my mother everything I did; she claimed that she would get in trouble if she did not tell. A typical older sister that thinks she is old enough to chastise me too.

My mother said, "Well, who is pregnant then because Jap (me) is a virgin."

Then I hear a pause, silence, and then my mother says, "Are you playing?"

My sister says, "No, I am not playing; you are going to be a grandmother."

I was so scared of what would happen next, and then I heard my mother's voice, "Jappppppppppp (that's my nickname), come in here!"

I started to cry so when she saw me she knew it was true. Then my mother starts to ask me a bunch of questions. I had a brain freeze, and I was stuck for words; I did not know what to say. But I needed to say something because I could see this was going to be a long night. I was crying, and my mother had no sympathy for me. She wanted to know facts and details. I told her I was pregnant by someone that was in the Military. I thought it would make things a little easier for me at home. Because first, I was so ashamed to tell her I was pregnant by Lil Reg, and second, I did not want to have to deal with the father thing right away. I did not have much information on the guy I told her I was pregnant by. Actually, I had never had sex with him. He was the boy my sister and I got in trouble for having in our house when my mother told us we could not have any company. My mother then called my uncle, who was in the service, to try and find this guy. I had not thought this thing through, and I was about to be caught.

Miz Melanie's Moments:
Here I am, repeating the cycle I had been through with my father without realizing it. I told my mother

that someone else was my baby's father like she told me. This is where I start to tell a bunch of lies that will later cause me a lot of problems. The truth will eventually come out.

My mother got on the phone and called her sisters because she discussed everything with her sisters. I was sitting in the living room crying while my mother was talking about me to her sisters. I hated my sister because she was the cause of all this. All night my mother fussed and cursed about having another mouth to feed. She said "I am not raising another child, and I don't know where you are going, but you are not brInging another child in here."

My mother went on and on, and I had to listen to her all night. When I finally fell asleep, it seemed as if I only slept for 10 minutes. The next morning I got up, took my shower, and got dressed for school.

I was just about to leave for school, and my mother called me and said, "Do Not Leave."

One of my aunts worked at a hospital in the city, and she had made me an emergency appointment. I just could not believe all of this had happened to my life this fast. At one point, no one paid any attention to me, and now I was the talk of the town. It seemed more like I was the laughing stock of the town. My mother was not talking too much this morning. I guess she got a lot out last night. She only spoke when she needed to. This is not good because this is now creepy and scary. We went to the doctor, and I was examined, and the doctor dropped another bomb. Now it's time to talk after the examination. My mother comes into the room, and the doctor tells her that I am seven and a half months pregnant and I would soon be eight months. All hell broke loose in that room.

My mother asked, "Eight months?" and the doctor said, "Yes, ma'am. Your daughter is almost eight months pregnant, according to the pelvic exam. Then the doctor said, "Where were you all this time that your daughter has been pregnant. And why did she wait until now to get prenatal care?"

Why did the doctor say that to my mother? That blew her top? My mother went crazy, and she cursed that doctor out. She told him not to ever speak to her in that manner again and that it was none of his fuckin' business. Then she looked at me and told me to "Come on, let's go."

I knew it was not over. I was going to get the backlash of this doctor's visit. I wanted to crawl under a rock and stay there. We were on the bus, and that seemed like the longest bus ride ever. When we arrived home, she told me to get something to eat. I thought it was over for the day. Then she started up again, "So, what are your plans for this baby because you are about to have the baby soon."

I said I didn't know, and why did I say that? I just did not know what to say at that moment. I did not want to be badgered again with this being pregnant stuff any longer. I was only 14 years old. How would I know what I was going to do? My life was a nightmare.

Going To School Pregnant

The best part of my days was going to school. It seemed like after my mother found out that I was pregnant, I blew up. My stomach was enormous, and everyone could tell that I was pregnant. Everybody in school was talking and whispering about me being pregnant. This was a new experience for the school. I never knew of any other person being pregnant at my high school. I had to go to the nurse after every class to make sure I was okay. I was really a liability in school. The school administrators didn't have a lot of these situations with young girls pregnant in school.

I am now an outcast in the school, and I am alone. It seemed like the friends I had before everyone knew I was pregnant were gone. Even though it was a lonely time, I would rather be in school and not at home. I started to hang out with this girl I met in the girl's bathroom. She was asking me about me being pregnant but little did I know that she too was pregnant. Nobody knew she was pregnant because she was not showing yet. I also started to hang out with this girl I knew from middle school. She was hanging with this new girl I met.

It made sense for all of us to hang out together. We started to confide in each other because we all seemed to be the school's outcasts. Me, Sabrina, and Cindy. Sabrina was the girl that was pregnant, and Cindy was dating an older guy. He was more like a grown man. They both asked me who I was pregnant by, and I told them I was pregnant by this guy in the military, telling my mother the same story. Sabrina was pregnant by a guy we went to school with, and they had just broken up. Sabrina was in love with him, but he thought he was God's gift to the girls. When she told him she was pregnant, he started to act funny with her.

Lil Reg went to the same school, and he happened to have a class with Sabrina and Cindy. He wanted to tell everybody that I was pregnant by him, but I did not want anybody to know. One reason was he was shorter than me, and nobody in school really knew him. This one particular day, I was in class, and when the bell for class to end rang, I saw all these people gathered outside of my class. I was always the last one to leave because I was moving slowly due to my belly being so big. When I came outside of my classroom, I saw Lil Reg, his best friend Ronnie, my two new best friends Sabrina and Cindy, in front of the crowd. Cindy was calling me, and she said, "Jap, this dude Lil Reg bet me a bag of weed that you are pregnant by him."

I was so caught off guard and embarrassed at the same time. Lil Reg and his friend were laughing hysterically, and I had the look of panic on my face. I just took off running down the hall chasing Lil Reg because I was now exposed in front of everybody in school. I could not believe he did that to me. While Lil Reg was running down the hall, he was yelling to Cindy, "Give me my bag of weed."

The school disciplinary teacher caught me running, and she screamed in a loud voice, calling my name, "Melanie Stroman, stop running right now!"

I stopped running, and she came over to talk to me with fear in her eyes. She said, "You can not be running in these halls pregnant you could have a major accident."

She took me to the nurse's office and told me to lie down for a half-hour. I was glad she did that because I needed to hide from the entire school for a minute. Then she allowed me to leave school early so I would not have to see the other students. Even with all that I had to go through that day, I still would rather be in school instead of being at home. I was miserable at home. A few days after the big announcement exposing who my baby father was, my mother got a phone call from Lil Reg's mother. I heard my mother responding to the conversation with aggression. I was instantly stressed because my mother's voice was elevated.

Lil Reg's father suggested that I get an abortion. He told my mother that I could go to New York and have a Therapeutic Abortion in which the doctor would insert a needle into my stomach, and the baby would be killed instantly and delivered vaginally. And that's when my mother's head came off, and she exploded. My mother used some words on him that I didn't even know existed. At that moment, she was so hurt, and I believed it was because she was fighting this battle alone.

I don't really know what happened and why my father was not in the picture. A few years earlier, my mother and father both sat me down and gave me the big announcement about him being my father. After my mother hung up that phone, she shouted at me all of the words that she didn't get to say to Lil Reg's father. My mother was heartbroken, disappointed, shocked, and defeated. Her daughter was pregnant at fourteen years old, almost eight months pregnant, and she was unaware. Not to mention that she wasn't sure who the baby's father was because her daughter (me) had lied the first time, and she was a single parent. Wow, that was a lot to be dealing with at one time from one child. I remember my mother just sobbing and saying she failed as a mother. As a mother, I don't know how I would have handled that pressure. My mother felt like I let her down, which I did. However, I was overlooked. I also felt like I didn't matter. I often felt like my mother thought I was okay and I didn't need too much attention.

Miz Melanie's Moments:
We, as parents, especially mothers, should always be in tune with our children. There are signs, but we have to see them; we must be able to read the room. In the time we live in now, it is extremely important to see signs in our children. We are living in a time when the kids don't talk due to electronics. Many of their feelings are kept in due to the silence of social media, where they can talk back through the computer. We must pay attention to mood swings,

changes in behavior, and if they become reserved or withdrawn. These are signs, and they are telling you that something is wrong.

My mother was dealing with her own issues in her personal life, trying to get ahead in life by furthering her education, the overhead of the household, and trying to raise her children. The burden was extremely heavy, and something went lacking. I fell through the cracks. My mother thought her children were alright; she felt like she had that on track. That is why communication is really important with you and your children. Talk to your children and tell them the truth. Be as honest as possible and tell them as much as you can. However, always remember they are your children and not your friend. You must set and keep boundaries. Boundaries teach respect, and children need to have respect. Respect and manners are mandatory. My mother was so mad with Lil Reg's family that she had forbidden me from talking to any of them. She told me not to let Lil Reg call or come over to her house.

Ever since my mother found out that I was pregnant, all I would do is cry. I cried every day during the last few months of my pregnancy. I am so blessed that I have a wonderful happy, beautiful daughter because she went through a lot in my womb. I was stressed in the first trimester, and the last of my term, I was depressed. I thank God for my blessing. I didn't go to school one day because I had a doctor's appointment. I had to go to the doctors twice a week because I hadn't had any prenatal care due to my mother finding out very late in my pregnancy.

Lil Reg called me to ask me how I was doing, and he asked me if he could come over to see me since I wasn't in school that day. I said, "Yes, you can come over before my mom gets home from work."

My mother was still at work, and I thought I could get him in and out before my mother came home. I really wanted to share these moments with Lil Reg, but I was afraid to feel those feelings or even show those feelings. I was not allowed to show that I felt that way. I had to feel the way that my mother felt because I lived at home with her. This day my mother came home from work a little early, and she rang the doorbell. We lived on the second floor of a two-story apartment building.

When my mother rang the bell, I knew it was her, and I panicked. I told Lil Reg and his friend that they had to leave right now because that's probably my mother. And my mother told me not to have you in her house. Lil Reg brought his friend because he was so proud to be a father in a few weeks. My mother pushed the elevator, and then she decided to walk up the steps, and she caught Lil Reg and his friend running down the steps. She was furious, and she punched and kicked him and his friend as they ran down the stairs. Lil Reg's friend fell down half of the steps, but he got up and kept running out of the building. When my mother came into the house, she was steaming and screaming at me.

I was sitting on a chair in the dining room. My mother was lamenting about how much stress I added to her life by bringing another mouth to feed in her house. And then she threw a pound of frozen bacon from the freezer at me. That bacon hit me in the head, and because I was so big and unbalanced from my stomach being so big, I fell on the floor. My mother's eyes got big as a basketball, and she rushed over to me and helped me up. She asked if I was okay, and she started to cry. She went into her bedroom and just sobbed.

I was so hardened because I was totally convinced that she did not like me, and I did not feel any remorse. I was angry with her because I felt like she was trying to kill my baby by knocking me out of the chair. Now that I am able to look at things from a different perspective, I now realize that she was overloaded with life and its circumstances. Before I got pregnant, my mother felt like she was just getting above water as a single parent. Things were finally starting to blossom for her. My mother was in school, and she was about to graduate. I am the youngest, and I was fourteen at the time. She was just about to be at the finish line because I was in junior high school. I was totally numb to how my mother was feeling, and I thought I hated her. Looking at things from her perspective, I now realize that she was stressed out about a lot of things.

Miz Melanie's Moments:
It's a struggle to raise a child, especially if you are raising the child alone. There are so many elements

to parenting, and you literally have to be extremely careful with every decision you make. Children are delicate, and they are a gift from God. Whatever we pour into them is what they will pour out. The challenge comes in handling and caring for the gift because life is not easy every day. Parents, we have the ability, authority, and the power to teach our children how to be the President of the United States of America or the prisoner doing life in prison. As parents, we teach our children to be the best they can be or the worst they can be. However, we are responsible for what we teach them and what their contribution will be to society. The decision starts at birth. Let's start making the right decisions for our children.

I Am About To Have A Baby

Ever since that day, my mother was really careful with how she handled me. She became really observant at every move that I made. She also didn't want me to go into labor, and she would not be there. When she would go over to her girlfriends to play cards, she would take me with her. One day she took me over to her girlfriend's house, and Big Momma was there. I went over to say hi to Big Momma and hug and kiss her. Big Momma said I looked like I was almost ready to have the baby because my stomach dropped. I had no clue as to what she was talking about.

She said, "you ain't no baby no more." I didn't know whether to smile in acknowledgment or to be mad because she was sarcastic. I just went to sit on the couch. Then Big Momma said to my mother, "Ain't no sense in you bringing her with you now. She's already pregnant. You should've been watching her before she got pregnant." And the entire table of adults busted out into laughter.

Big Momma was always saying something sarcastic. She would say things that were true, but you didn't want to hear. Everywhere my mother went, I had to go with her. Sometimes my mother would be out overnight. Those are the times when I really wanted to be home in bed. Because I was so close to my due date, my mother did not want me to go into labor at home alone. I was so big that the school asked my mother to keep me at home because I was a liability to the school.

They did not have a plan in place for pregnant teenage girls. The school dean kept a very close watch on me while I was in school, and most days, she released me early to catch the bus before all the other students were released.

My older cousin had given me all of her maternity clothes from her recent pregnancy. This was her and her husband's first child. She had really nice and expensive maternity clothes. I had so many clothes, and people would tell me that I looked nice in them. I was wearing my regular clothes before my cousin gave me her maternity clothes. I could hardly zip my pants up because I was so big. My mother gave me a baby shower, and only my side of the family was invited. She did not invite Lil Reg's family because she hated them, and she would always say they wanted to kill the baby.

My mother gave me a shower to help with the things I would need for the baby when she was born. I had nothing, and the baby was going to be here soon. Everyone that attended the shower bought really nice gifts. My godmother gave me her crib from the birth of her son. I had so many gifts, and I was thankful. These gifts alleviated a lot of pressure off of my mother, and that made me even happier. I don't want people to think that my mother was a monster, although she could be at times. These were the results of mistakes and decisions that she made for her family. She wanted the best for her children, and she did what she thought was right. When she made a mistake or a bad decision, she did not feel like she should explain herself to her children. And that is halfway correct.

Miz Melanie's Moments:
When a parent makes a mistake or a bad decision, it's good to acknowledge it, own it. Be brave and apologize if necessary. Let your child know that you are human and you make mistakes. Let them know that the mistake was not intentional. Children are built to love their parents no matter what. Even if you find yourself on drugs, an alcoholic, mental health issues, whatever condition you are in, your children will still love you. However, our children just want us as parents to show them that their feelings are important and that their feelings matter.

The Big Day

Today is the big day. I went into labor, but I didn't know I was in labor. I was now fifteen and about to have my baby. I remember feeling a lot of pain in my abdominal area and trying not to let it show. My mother asked me in an elevated voice, "are you in labor?"

I replied, "I don't know, but my stomach is hurting.

She said, "Hurry up and take a shower so we can go to the hospital."

When I think back on that day, that was the wrong day to be taking a shower while in labor. So much could have gone wrong. I could have had the baby in the shower. My mother always told me to make sure I showered and had on clean underwear before going to the doctor or hospital. I went to the hospital, and they said they needed to keep me because I was dilated five centimeters. I had no clue what they were talking about. It actually meant that I was halfway there. I needed to be ten centimeters to be fully dilated and give birth. I just wanted something for the pain.

When I got a few more centimeters, they gave me an epidural in my spine. The doctor told me if I moved, I would be paralyzed from the waist down for the rest of my life. I was so scared, but I tried to stay very still, even though I was having contractions. Then after the pain subsided, I had to walk until the baby was ready to come. After hours of labor, I delivered a big healthy baby girl 8lbs. 9ozs. 22 inches long.

I had a big baby at fifteen years old. I loved her at first sight. She was the best thing that ever happened to me. I was so proud of her. She came into the world absolutely perfect. I prayed, and I asked God to allow my baby girl to love me. I needed someone to love me unconditionally, to love me for me. And God answered that prayer immediately. Because she absolutely loves me to pieces, her and her sisters.

Miz Melanie's Moments:
I was fifteen years old, and I had a baby. I am still being taught about life, and I now have a life to teach. I didn't have anything to teach her because I am still learning. All I knew about being a mother was to feed her when she was hungry, change her when she was wet, bathe her and dress her up in pretty clothes.

Lil Reg came up to see me in the hospital, so I thought. He went to see the baby first. I guess he wanted to make sure the baby was really his baby since I said he was not the original father. It takes me back to when I was born. I was told someone else was my father. Look at how cycles repeat themselves if not broken. He was so happy because not only did the baby look just like him; she was also born on his birthday. What an amazing birthday present. He came to thank me for such a beautiful baby girl. It was an awesome day.

Finally, I was experiencing some happiness in my life due to the birth of my baby girl. The reality of me actually having a baby finally hit me. My life has changed forever. God had blessed me with my first adult assignment, my baby. I had to stay in for a month because Big Momma was ole school, and she did not allow me to get right back to life as normal. You had to heal first. She told me I was still open and I could have a prolapse. I had no clue what she was talking about, but I had to abide by her rules.

I couldn't wait to get back to some type of normal living, like going outside. After my six-week check-up, I was able to get my new life started. I would get up for school, and I had to get myself and my baby dressed. Lil Reg's aunt would come to pick the baby and me up every morning and take us to her house. Lil Reg's grandmother, Nanny, watched the baby, and I went to school. After school, I would come to pick the baby up. Lil Reg's Aunt would come home from work, cook dinner, feed us, and take us home. That was my routine every day from Monday through Friday.

Lil Reg instantly became popular in school. The entire school was congratulating him on being a new father. We were a couple for a few months until I started getting so much attention from guys I never thought would have given me the time of day. Lil Reg also got extremely popular because he now had a kid. He was popular with the girls, too. However, I did not care because he was not on my level anymore. I was no longer interested because I started going out with my childhood crush. I always wanted to go out with him, but I thought he was a square. Suddenly he was very attractive to me, and I wanted to be with him. That was probably because I was now having sex, and my grown woman hormones kicked in.

I'm Feeling Myself

Melvin, my childhood crush, is now my new boyfriend. His family would always tease me because they thought we were together before we got together. So now that I was really with him, the jokes got worse. They would joke that Melvin was my baby's father, and they laughed about that for years. I would be over at Melvin's house, and when his mother would go in her room, Melvin and I would go in his room. I loved Melvin, and I didn't let anything stop me from going to his house every weekend. We had passionate sex, but again I was having unprotected sex. I was on birth control pills, but I was not responsible, and I did not take them every morning. Sometimes I would forget, and after three months of dating Melvin, I was pregnant again. I was devastated, and I knew this time I was in bigger trouble. I wasn't stable with the first baby at home, and I knew I could not go home with a second baby. My baby was not even two years old yet, and here I am, pregnant again.

Miz Melanie's Moments:
My mother was not aware of how and even if I was taking my birth control pills. I was given a prescription for them every time I went to the clinic. However, I was not responsible enough to take care of a baby, so I was even more incompetent to take medication. These are the things that parents are supposed to be on top of with their children. When

I DECIDED TO LAUGH

you become a parent, you are a parent for the rest of your life. This job is a lifelong assignment. Mothers, fathers, parents, this job does not come with a manual or actual expiration date; it's on-the-job training. However, you can make it, and you can actually do a great job. However, You must learn from every mistake. Just don't repeat the mistakes. Please don't allow your mistakes to become habitual.

I never told Melvin or anyone else that I was pregnant. I only told my girlfriend, Sabrina. She told me about a doctor that I could go to to get an abortion. I set up the appointment, and I had to go on a Friday. I asked my mother if I could go over to Sabrina's house for the weekend, and she said yes. I took my baby to Sabrina's house, and I went to the hospital. My mother had no clue as to what I was having done or where I was at. The doctor was Dr. Bruce Burger, and he assured me that I was going to be okay. I did not need my mother's permission to have the procedure done. I was there all weekend and released on Sunday. I was all alone, by myself.

Miz Melanie's Moments:
This was awful on so many levels. This is why communication with your children is so important. I could have hemorrhaged and bled to death, and my mother would not have known anything. I was sixteen, and I did not know what the procedure this doctor was doing on me. Sure, he talked to me about

the procedure and gave me some paperwork to sign, but I could not comprehend those medical terminologies. I could have been a ginny pig for some experiment the doctor was doing. I was absolutely clueless. I was scared of the procedure's outcome, but I was more scared to tell my mother that I was pregnant again. All I knew was that I could not go home pregnant again. Fear will make a person do things that could change your life forever and possibly cost you your life. No child should ever be so scared to talk to their parents. If I were in communication with my mother, this would not have ever happened. What I needed was for my mother to say after the birth of my first child, "You have made one mistake now; let's talk and make sure you don't make any more mistakes." When your child messes up or makes a mistake, reach out to help your child. Don't leave your child to rely on their own abilities. They are operating from a small range of experience. I was not responsible. I was unable to make sound decisions. I was operating out of hurt and pain. I was a wild child, reckless and rebellious. I was incapable of making sound adult decisions for my life. I was murdering a child! That right there tells you that I was not responsible.

I could have died on that operating table at the same time. But thanks be to God for His grace and His mercy! I purposely made sure that I talked about this because things like this are happening to our children every day because they are afraid to talk to their parents. They feel like they will be condemned, criticized, ostracized, and chastised. I am not saying we do not chastise our children for making bad choices and mistakes. I am not saying we do not reprimand our children for doing wrong. I am saying that there are ways to do things that will get your children to see the bigger picture. There are ways to show your children that you want the best for them; you want them to win. One of the hardest things to do when you have to chastise your children is to get them to understand that you love them. Making your children understand that there are consequences to every wrong action. My consequence for getting pregnant was I could have died getting that abortion. I am not proud of what I did, and I am not glamorizing this fact. I still hurt from that dumb mistake. I am not lucky , I am forgiven. God watched over me in my weakness and my stupidity. Thank you, Jesus, for not giving me what I deserved in that situation.

I hope this can help parents see the importance of having a great relationship and keep the communication window open between you and your children. Talking to your children is healthy and refreshing. It builds great relationships with you and your children. Remember, if you have more than one child, have individual conversations, private, confidential conversations. They are not all the same. They are individuals. Build a different relationship with each of your children separately. I believe I have a great relationship with my children, but there are still some things we can work on. There are still some things that they do not talk to me about. They may talk to their siblings or their girlfriends. That's where my prayer life goes into effect.

I ask God to be the mother, father, sister, or friend to them that they need whenever they do not feel like they can talk to me. Also, parents, God will show you things to pray for in your prayer time, and He will give you words to say to your children. One of our main jobs as a mother is to pray for our children. Parents, we are not always going to get everything RIGHT! We are not perfect! We are going to make mistakes. But, it's what you do after the mistake that is effective. This is not an excuse. This is my truth. Also, my mother should have known about this decision that I made. It was fear that kept me from telling her. My mother did not deserve to be treated like she didn't exist in my life. That was a completely wrong decision on my part.

It still hurts me that I did not tell my mother about this situation. She probably would have put that doctor's practice out of business. I remember leaving the hospital and feeling so drained, but I had to act normal so that my mother would not have noticed anything unusual. I went over to Sabrina's house and picked up my baby, and I went home. Luckily, when I arrived home, nobody was home, so I could rest a little before everyone got home.

I had to get up and go to school the next morning, and I could hear Big Mama's voice saying, "you can't go outside after you have a child. You could have a prolapse." I was hoping and praying that I did not have a prolapse. That would have been a dead giveaway. Dr. Bruce Burger gave me birth control pills and condoms to prevent another pregnancy. I believed that I had learned a valuable lesson because I probably took two pills a day after that weekend. Again I don't know if I was taking the right birth control pills for my body type. All I know is I was taking these pills to prevent another pregnancy. That should have been enough to stop me from having sex, but that was the only way I knew to show a guy that I loved him.

Too, Too Grown

Shortly after that, I stopped seeing Melvin because I met this new guy named Danny. He was so cute, and he was attracted to me. When I was with my girlfriends, he came up to me in school and told me he would be my next boyfriend. I was flabbergasted, excited, and ecstatic all at the same time. For that moment, I felt pretty and attractive. All of my girlfriends were cheering me on, saying, "Girl, don't let him go."

I was still going with Melvin, but the fire was gone in that relationship after I had the abortion. I don't know what happened, but I distanced myself from Melvin. One day after school, I walked to the bus stop another way with Danny, and Melvin showed up. Somebody told him that I was seeing Danny. Melvin walked up, and Danny and I were holding hands. Melvin was a non-confrontational guy, so he just looked at me and kept going.

After that, I just kind of hid from him because I could not face him. Danny and I became an item instantly. I started going over to Sabrina's house every weekend now that she had her baby. I was worry-free when I went over to her house. She had a lot of siblings, and they were the typical family. They loved one another, they argued, they had to clean up that big house, they would sing and dance together, they had to babysit the younger kids. It was always a joy, laughter mixed with a little dysfunction in their home, but I loved it there. I longed for that, and I would go over there every chance I could. I also loved going over to Sabrina's house because her entire family would help me with my baby.

One night my baby was crying all night, and I gave her a bottle. I bathed her and made sure she had a clean diaper, and she still would not stop crying. I was crying because I did not know what to do. Sabrina's mother came into the room and told me to give her the baby. She started to rub on my baby's gums with her finger. She told me that the baby was teething. I had no clue what teething was. All I knew was my baby would not stop crying. She told me to put her teething ring in the freezer and let the baby suck on it when it got frozen. Sabrina's older sister came and got the baby for the rest of the day. That made me feel loved and cared for. They took the time to help me and teach me what to do with my baby, and that's what I needed. I guess my mother let me go over to Sabrina's house to get a break from the responsibility of my baby and me.

Miz Melanie's Moments:
Parents, we have to make sure that we are not alienating our children with the punishment when we are chastising. My mother was trying to teach me a lesson, but I did not need a lesson at that point. I had already had the lesson. I needed to be taught how to take care of this baby. This was not a babydoll. I had the real thing. Each child is different, and you have to parent each child differently. I was

drawn to Sabrina's s house because what I needed to be taught as a new mother, I was getting from Sabrina's mother and family. We have to be able to distinguish the needs of each child. I made a mistake due to other things going on with me that were not detected before this happened. This is a chain reaction to so many other things that my mother was not even aware of. That is why it is extremely important to be observant and notice everything you can about your children and how they develop.

My mother was hard on me, but she loved my baby. She said she was too young to be called grandma, so she gave herself the name Gammy. And every night when she came home, she would say Gammy home, and my baby would look for her and smile. I wished we had a better relationship. I wish I could talk to her now about my trauma, what I was feeling, and tell her about the things that happened to me. Danny and I became inseparable. I started spending every moment with Danny that I could. I stopped going over to Sabrina's house. Danny was a great kisser and dancer.

We used to go out dancing every Saturday night at a club called the Astro Disc. This was a club for teenagers, and it was open every weekend for dancing. Danny could dance. He was in a dance group, and they went to different places to dance. My mother thought I was over at Sabrina's house, but I would go to Danny's house for the weekend. His mother worked most weekends, and after work, she would stay over at her boyfriend's house.

Danny hung out with this boy named Josh. He was older than Danny, and he, too, was a part of the dance group. He influenced Danny because he had money and his own apartment. I was so overwhelmed with home, the baby, and the fact that I was always in trouble. I just could never get things right at home. My mother despised me because of the baby. She vowed not to make my life easy because she said I would not bring another baby into her house. She was always yelling and complaining about everything. I had to wake up every morning at 5:30 to get the baby ready.

My mother would say to me, "when you are a mother, you have to get up early and tend to your child." I felt like she was torturing me. I had to get me, and the baby's clothes ready the night before I couldn't even watch television. I had to make the baby's bottles and ensure everything she would need during the day was in the bag. My mornings were hectic. Most mornings, I would get a cuss out, and a door slam on her way out. My mother was very angry with me, and she showed it every single day. Today I probably would ask for us to go to counseling because the punishment was too harsh. My mother's reasoning for giving me tough love was to teach me that raising a child is not easy. I get my mother's reasoning, but she forgot to add some sugar to the mix. It was a bitter situation at all times. She never asked if I needed a break or offered to watch the baby while I went out with girlfriends.

Everything was like I was in the military, and she was the sergeant. I just needed a break, a getaway, and I finally found one. I would drop the baby off every day at Lil Reg's aunt's house and meet Danny at Josh's house. I would skip school and smoke weed, and lay around with Danny until it was time to go and pick up my baby. I needed to have some peace before I went home. I was not happy at home. I tried to be at home as little as possible. My mother had no idea that I was not going to school. She whooped me when she found out that I had failed the 11th grade. I failed because I was not going to school, and I didn't care; that was the scary part. But little did I know I would get a lesson about life shortly down the road.

Miz Melanie's Moments:
Parents make sure that you are aware of your children 's progress in school. We go to school to get the skills and education we need to be successful and navigate the world. School also teaches social skills that we need in our future lives and careers. I missed that opportunity, and I had to go back to school later in life. I did not get my high school diploma until I was fifty years old. I had to get that because I had made it mandatory in my household that my children could not come out of school until they had a Bachelor's Degree. I had the hardest time getting a job without a high school diploma. By this time in my life, after the birth of my baby, my mother probably checked out. She probably was tired of caring about the weight of my situation.

And that's easy to do when you have stuff going on in your own life that you are trying to overcome. But the key is to stay focused. If your child is not going to school, you should know about that. I don't know if the school called and just did not get a response or if the school just wrote me off. Whatever the reason, my mother should have been notified that I was not in school. Parents, check your children's grades weekly or monthly. Call their teacher and speak with them. Set up meetings to talk about what your child needs to succeed. Ask if there is anything your child should be improving in. Go to every parent-teacher meeting.

Parents, it is our job to make our children know that they are our priority. It is our job to let them know how important an education is. It is our job to build their self-esteem, letting them know they can be whatever they want to be in life and that they can achieve whatever goals they set for themselves. Let your children know that they can reach the top of the sky. Let your children know that they have your undivided attention and your support. Your support and attention mean the world to your children. They can reach the highest mountain with you there cheering them on. I can't say this or stress this enough. We must make our children know they are the most important people in our world and that they matter. My middle daughter got left down in the third grade. It was not because she was not smart. In fact, she is super intelligent; she could have taught the class that showed how advanced she was. She needed to know all of her timetables to advance to the fourth grade. But she would not learn these times tables, and I could not figure out why. I painted the entire time's tables from one to ten times tables on her walls in big blue numbers in her room. Every time she opened her eyes and was in her room, she had no other choice but to look at and memorize those times tables. However, that was not the answer to her problem because she knew the timetables. She had trauma that she could not verbalize. The trauma affected her so bad it crippled her ability to translate what was happening. Her cousin, her best friend, had died suddenly. They were in the same kindergarten class, and they went to the same daycare after school every day. My daughter did not understand, and she did not know how to make it make sense. When a child has trauma, it triggers toxic stress in the brain. It cripples and debilitates their emotions. Childhood trauma makes a child fall into depression, gives them anxiety, and can turn them into antisocial people. And that's what happened to my daughter. However, I did not know that was what she was dealing with at the time.

Danny and I started having sex. I was Danny's first, and I had no idea of that fact. He later told me that I was his first about twenty years later. Danny wanted me to be with him every second of the day. I love that because he was showing me that he cared about me. I longed for someone, especially a man, to feel that way about me. I started staying the night every weekend with Danny. Then I started staying until the middle of the week before I would come home. When I came home after being over to Danny's house for days, my mother would whoop my behind severely. But, I didn't care because, after a few days, I would go back again. And this kept happening until she put me out with my baby.

I'm Almost Grown

O ne time I just left home because I was tired of my mother and her rules. I have a baby now, and I needed my mother to understand that. Plus, I felt like I was almost grown anyway. I told my friend Spankie that I was tired of my mother and I wanted to leave. So he asked his mother if I could rent a room from her. Spankie did not live with his mother because he did not like the man that she was dating. So he moved in with his father because his mother moved the man she was dating into the house. His mother was a pastor, and she was very religious. She would have Bible Study and Prayer in her home, and he was embarrassed about that too.

His mother said I could rent a room from her until I could find my own place. I was only seventeen years old at the time. I had a job at a black-owned well-established restaurant in our neighborhood. That restaurant was where all of the black city officials and dignitaries came to eat and do business. The entertainers that came to town came there to eat too. Tobbins Inn was known all over the tri-state area. Everybody who was somebody ate at that restaurant. From the regular people to the well-established. That's the same restaurant my mother and father took me to tell me the truth about my paternity.

Mr. and Mrs. Tobbin were all business, and they did not play. If they gave you a job, they expected you to work. I worked there for a few months. I remember working on the night of my senior prom. I did not attend the prom because I had gotten left down. Almost everybody that went to the prom that night came to the restaurant to eat after the prom. I was humiliated and embarrassed. I am serving them when I should have been amongst them. People were telling me how great of a time that they had, and everyone looked so nice. I wanted to crawl under a rock.

I heard people were talking about me because I had dropped out of school and now I am working in a bar and restaurant. I didn't know which was worse between living with Spankie's mother and working at Tobbins Inn. But it was better than living with my mother because I seemingly did what I wanted to do. I was so defiant that I didn't care about the consequences. I did not want to live by my mother's rules. I did not care what my mother would do to me because I was numb. I wanted to live in a world where I was free from all the cares of this world.

When I worked, my aunt watched my daughter, and it was very convenient because my aunt lived around the corner from Spankie's mother's house. I was grateful that Spankie's mother let me rent a room from her, but she was annoying. She talked about Jesus and the Bible all the time. She wanted me to come to prayer and Bible study in her home, and I did not feel like that. I was miserable working at Tobbins Inn because I did not want to be chastised at work, and Mr. and Mrs. Tobbin were constantly chastising me.

Mrs. Tobbin would always say to me, "you think you're grown." I felt like I was grown because I worked and I was renting a room. So, I started looking for another job because working there was like living at home with my mother. I got hired at the famous Stenton Diner. Everybody in the city came there after a night out on the town.

After the bar and the after-hour spot closed, you came to the Stenton Diner to eat. I got hired for the graveyard shift; that's the overnight shift. I took this shift so that I could be home with my baby during the day. My aunt watched her overnight, and she went to daycare for a few hours during the day so that I could sleep. My life was hectic. I met a big sister and mentor at the diner. She taught me the ropes and how to be fast and make tips. I really looked up to her because she really looked out for me.

When men would come into the restaurant and give me a hard time, she would go over to the table and stand up for me. She was really cool, and I needed someone like that in my life to cover me while I was going through this storm. There were two guys that came in every weekend, and they knew her and were cool with her. They were her regulars.

One morning after work, she invited the two guys and me over to her apartment. We went over there to party. She had drinks, weed, cocaine, food, music, whatever you wanted. They were snorting the cocaine, and I was mostly drinking and smoking the weed. Then we coupled up, she was with one of the guys, and I was with the other guy. She went into her room with her guy and me, and my guy went into her spare room. They all were in their late twenties, and I was only seventeen years old.

I had consensual sex with my guy. I don't remember his name, and I don't even remember what he looks like. I fell asleep, and when I woke up, I woke up to my big sister, my mentor, having oral sex with me. The guy was gone, and I was left naked from the encounter he and I had. I was horrified. I was being molested all over again, but this time by a woman. I remember just lying there stiff, like when Mr. Raymond was raping me. The tears just rolled down my face like they did when Mr. Raymond was raping me.

I was devastated because she was my friend, my big sister, someone I trusted, and she betrayed me too. I could not believe that this was happening to me. I could not believe she did this. After she was done raping me, I got up and got dressed, and left.

I walked to Spankie's mother's house, and that was about 50 blocks from that apartment. I cried and talked to God, asking him what was wrong with me; why was everybody always taking advantage of me? Why did she rape me, too? Why didn't I matter? Why didn't anyone care about me? Why did people treat me like trash? Why wasn't I worth anything? Why didn't I have any value?

I despised that woman, my so-called big sister, after that. When I walked away that day, I never looked back. I never went back to that job at the diner, and I never saw her again. If I had to identify her in a lineup, I could not tell you what she looked like or her name. But I do remember where she lived, and that apartment building is still there, but it is abandoned. I never told anybody about what she did to me. I put it in a compartment and never opened it until I started writing this book.

Miz Melanie's Moments:
I struggled with whether or not I would disclose this in this book because I had never told anyone this story. The only people that knew were me and her and the Lord. But I didn't want to reveal this for a few reasons. 1. I hadn't told my daughters about this horrific experience. 2. I was ashamed that I was molested/raped by a woman. 3. I felt dumb and stupid that this happened to me at an older age. 4. I felt responsible for this happening to me. But as I was writing the book, the Lord told me to reveal it. The Lord told me to tell the testimony so that someone else could get free. I also struggled because I didn't know what to say if I was to tell someone. I wondered if I had caused this to happen to me. I wondered why I did not tell her to stop or why I didn't kick her in the face. I wondered why I was just silent. I had become that same little girl again. Writing this book made me go back to the scene of the crime to face it so that God could fix it. Also, I needed to explain to single mothers / single parents/co-parents and all parents that this is what could happen to your child when you neglect them or give up on them or turn a blind eye or a deaf ear. Things happen in the streets, that's why it's important to talk to your children. It's important to

have a relationship with your children. I can't stress the importance of building a relationship enough. The streets are waiting to get a hold of our children. My mother is deceased, and she never knew this happened to me. Another time I could have been killed, and my mother wouldn't have known what was happening.

Shortly after that experience, I left Spankie's mother's house. I was wounded badly, and I could not hear anything Spankie's mother had to say about God. I felt like God didn't care about me either when I was being raped and molested.

My First Apartment

I started staying over at Danny's house every day. Danny's mother and siblings were tired of my baby and me staying at their house. People get tired of you after a while of you living in their space. Danny and I got a job at this dye factory making good money. Then we found an apartment up the street from his mother's house.

The owner of the factory liked Danny, and he gave him an opportunity to be a manager. He met another guy there who was also a manager and had a good reputation because his mother worked for the owner for years. They had that place jumping. They mixed the different dyes, so they were important to the company. The company had a big contract with the Danskin Company, which sold dance apparel. Danny would steal about ten Danskin's in all colors a night. And then he started a side business. I had every color and style of Danskin that there was.

Danny made good money from his new business. People were always calling and coming over to his mother's house to buy a Danskin. We bought a car and Danny taught me how to drive. I didn't even have a driver's license, but I was on the road. We rented our apartment from this guy who was buying the building. It was a duplex, so he was using our rent to pay the mortgage. We were so young and dumb, but we had our own apartment and our own car.

Danny's father lived down in Jacksonville, Florida, and he asked Danny to come down to Florida to help him out with his business. Danny wanted to leave and start over new because he felt guilty about stealing the garments from the company. So, he moved to Florida with his father and left my baby and me alone in the apartment.

I had an apartment and a car at seventeen years old. I was happy that I had a car and an apartment, but the apartment had mice. The landlord did not have a solution to getting rid of them. He told me to invest in a cat. I am not a cat person, but I had to get a cat because I was scared the mice would bite my daughter and me. I didn't grow up in a house with mice, which was my major turn-off with the apartment.

I would take my daughter to daycare and go to work every day. I would go to Sabrina's house and stay on the weekends because they had an after-hour spot that opened every weekend. The party was always a good time. I loved being there and out on my own. I rarely had communication with my mother except when she wanted to see the baby. I stopped seeing Lil Reg's family too. They were not stepping up to the plate to help me with housing, so I did not keep in touch with them too much. However, Lil Reg's mother gave me a credit card for the baby to buy her clothes. I could use a credit card every month, and that was a great help. I ruined it when I purchased clothes for me on the card, and Lil Reg's mother stopped the card. She told me she was buying clothes for the baby, not for me. She told me that my mother should make sure I had clothes, not her.

My life was seemingly going well, but I hated the landlord. It seemed like when he noticed that Danny was no longer at the apartment, he started treating me badly. But I had no clue that it wasn't because Danny was no longer there; it was because he was having problems keeping the property. Sometimes I would come home, and the lights would be off, and he would say it was a blackout in the building, but it was because he did not pay the light bill. He would give me a candle and tell me the problem should be fixed by the next day. I sometimes did not have heat or hot water because he was not paying the bills. It was horrible, but I had my own place.

It was dark and gloomy there, and I really did not want to stay there after a while. He also would charge me different amounts for the rent sometimes by lying about what needed to be done in my apartment. I paid the money because I needed my apartment and I did not know what he was doing was illegal. I talked to Sabrina's mother about how I was being treated at the apartment. Ms. Dee told me to come live with them at her house because my landlord took advantage of me. I was so happy because I loved it over her house. She treated me like one of the family. She taught me things I needed to know about being a mother. She would talk to me when I had questions, and she was easy to talk to.

Ms. Dee set me up to get public assistance, food stamps, and a medical card for me and my baby. Of course, I had to pay rent and give her my food stamps for food. She would ask me what I wanted when she went to the store. She made sure if I wanted a particular item, she would make sure that she purchased it for me.

I had chores like all of the other family members. I probably did more than everybody else because I wanted to be a part of this family. I admired their family bond, and I wanted to be as much a part of this family as all the other family members. Then something major happened, and I was forced to leave. My mother found out that I was on public assistance, and she blew her top. She called Ms. Dee and told her that she would send the police over to her house and have her arrested for harboring a minor. She was really mad because she had hooked me up with public assistance. My mother was getting assistance for my daughter, but she could not get it for me because I was still a minor, and I was on her job's medical plan.

The problem with this entire situation was I did not know that my mother was getting assistance for my baby. I believe my mother should have had some kind of conversation with me, letting me know these things. My mother told me that I would be a bum, just like all of Ms. Dee's kids. My mother told me that she never raised me on public assistance and that I would not raise my child on public assistance. My mother was furious, and I had to feel all of that frustration.

Ms. Dee told me that I had to leave because my mother was threatening her, and she was just trying to help me. I was so embarrassed because Ms. Dee was helping me, and she opened her door for my daughter and me when we had nowhere to go. The real reason was the state discontinued my mother's claim and assisted me directly. My mother came over to Ms. Dee's house, picked my baby and me up, and took us back home. However, that didn't last too long. My mother was living with her boyfriend, and I felt like she did not want me to be there.

I was looking for a job and applying for a school. I was lucky to get into a dental assistant program. I started taking my daughter back to daycare, and I was going to school. I thought I was on the right track. I was finally doing something with my life to make my mother proud. One night I was home doing my hair for school the next day. I had given my baby a bath, and she was in bed. Our clothes and bags were ready for us to get up and leave the next morning as part of our routine. My mother and her boyfriend came home, and they had a huge fight. It was a bad fight, and my mother was acting really strange.

She goes into my room and locks the door. Her boyfriend tells me that my mother took some pills to kill herself, and she was locked in my room. I was frantic, and I went to the door to call my mother, and she would not respond. I was crying, and I kept begging my mother to open the door. Her boyfriend told me to try to get the door open, and I got a screwdriver and opened the door. My mother was furious with me for opening the door. She told me that I was helping her boyfriend kill her. It was evident that they both had entirely too much to drink that night. Both of them were acting strange due to the amount of alcohol they both consumed.

My mother got up and told me that I had one hour to get my things and get out. I started to cry because now my baby was awake, and she was crying too. My mother told me that I am the cause of the boyfriend getting access to her and I had to go tonight. I could not believe what had just happened. I called Sabrina and asked her if I could come over, and she said yes. It was 3:00 in the morning. My sister's boyfriend came to pick me up, and he took me over to Sabrina's house. I was there for a few days before Sabrina's mother asked me what my plans were. She said she did not want to have me over at her house, and have my mother come to her house threatening her again. I did understand what she was saying, and I asked her if she could please allow me and my baby to stay there. I did not have a room the first couple of weeks I was there. So, I lived out of a closet. I had all of my things and my baby in a closet.

Later Ms. Dee gave me my own room. She said I was paying rent and I needed my own room. Things were looking up for me. I was in a trade school, and I was getting assistance from the state. I woke up every morning and took my baby to daycare, and I went to school. Ms. Dee did not like that I would take my baby to daycare. She felt like I should leave my baby there with all the other kids. I never wanted my baby to be a burden on anybody. My mother had drilled in my head "That is your baby, take care of your baby," and I never wanted anyone to say I left my baby on them.

On the weekends, I would hustle my weed at Ms. Dee's after-hour spot. One day, coming home from picking my baby up from daycare, I noticed this rust-colored car was following me. The man inside of the car kept calling me, but I ignored him. He asked me if I wanted a ride, and I said no. This man would wait for me every day at the same time and follow me in his car. This particular day he got out of the car and approached me. He introduced himself to me and asked me my name. He told me his name was John, and I asked to see his identification because I thought he was lying.

I called him Mr. John, and he did not like that. He said just call me John. He asked me if he could give me a ride. He said that he had seen us walking for a few weeks and wanted to help. Immediately Mr. John got my attention. I needed help, and now he was speaking my language. I was fully aware of what he wanted for the help. He gave me a ride, and he met me every day for about a month and drove me to Sabrina's house. I would always get out of his car around the corner because I did not want anybody to see me with this old man.

The first day he dropped me off, he gave me a hundred-dollar bill. That money was like a million dollars to me at that time. He was reeling me into his trap. Then he started taking me to really nice restaurants to eat. Every restaurant was far away because he was married. He owned a travel agency, and his business was lucrative at that time. He gave me money at the end of every week for my baby and me.

Now the time had come for me to do my part. I had to have sex with this man. It was the same experience that I had when I was being molested as a child. The only difference was I was older, and I had given my consent. I would lay there until he was finished having sex with me, and I would hold my lips tight when he would kiss me. I just wanted it to be over quickly so that I could go.

Miz Melanie's Moments:
I found myself in another situation, and in my weakest time, this man appeared. Because of my situation, I was drawn to Mr. John for help. I was a young girl trying to navigate these streets without much parental guidance. I was rebellious with built-up anger, which caused me to be unable to hear anything that my mother was trying to teach me. Parents, do not throw your children away. Find the place of comfortability in the relationship with your children, which will lay the foundation for deep, honest conversation. Sometimes the conversation will get emotional but do not allow the conversation to get combative or let the anger come in. Remember, parents - you set the tone of every conversation. Our children move off of our energy.

Things were going well until Sabrina started to get jealous of my popularity. I had money, I was in a trade school, but I had no stability in my life. I didn't have the family bond that she had with her family. I would try to do whatever I could to stay in Sabrina's good graces because I was there due to us being friends. When Mr. John would give me money, I would buy all the kids in the house some things. But things just got worse between us, and she stopped speaking to me. Sabrina felt like I thought I was better than her. I did not think I was better than her, but I always wanted more than what I had.

I always knew that I was an outsider, and that was her family. Families always stick together no matter what happens. Sabrina wanted me to leave and Ms.Dee said I did not have to leave because I paid rent to live there. But Sabrina made it difficult for me to stay there. The atmosphere was hostile, and it felt different when I would come home from school. I had started to buy her acceptance because I did not want to be told to leave.

I started talking to my mother on the phone, and I told her that Sabrina would break into my room and steal my money and clothes. My mother told the baby and me to come home. My mother told me that "When you have children, you will do things in life that you never thought you would do to take care of your children. She told me my father was concerned about my baby and me, and he wanted to see us. My father came over to Sabrina's house and told me to get my things because he was taking me home.

I felt so good that day. My father had actually come to pick me up and rescue me, something I had longed for most of my life. I remember getting my things feeling a sense of protection. I felt at that moment like my father loved and cared about me. He took me back to my mother's house, where I stayed until Danny returned from Florida.

Move Supporter

I left my mother's house and went to stay with Danny at his mother's house again. This time we were renting a room from his mother. I hung out with Danny's little sister; we both went to school in Center City and would meet up for lunch. One day we were meeting up for lunch, and we saw this crowd of protesters of all races outside of City Hall. We became intrigued by what they were saying, and we started to meet there every day for lunch. The protestors that were speaking were Move Supporters. They were protesting the injustice done to the Move 9.

Miz Melanie's Moments:
Move is an organization in Philadelphia that was founded by a man named John Africa. The movement was originally a Christian movement for Life. The organization advocates for nature laws and natural living. When I became affiliated with the Move Organization, it was because of the brutal beating of Delbert Africa and the mass incarceration of 9 Move people. I was an active Move Supporter up until a few months after I had my second daughter. I was easily influenced, and I got caught up with the organization without fully knowing the cause they were fighting for. I will always love The Move Organization because they are some of the nicest and caring people I know. They covered me and made me feel like part of the

family when I was going through my situation. It seems like I was looking for family and love all of my life, and I come from an enormous family.

It was amazing to see how people came together to protest this outrageous mass incarceration of Move 9. We both were super impressionable, and we got caught up fast. I started going to the protest every day, and then I eventually stopped going to school to be an active Move Supporter. Danny and I started having problems because he did not like me hanging out with the organization. I eventually started staying overnight. I took my daughter out of daycare and kept her with me all day, every day.

Shortly after that, I moved in with other Move Supporters. It was easy for me to decide to move in with the other supporters because I was always looking for a stable home for me and my daughter. All of this had transpired in my life, and I wasn't even twenty years old. I began supporting the Move 9 at court. I really didn't know the root of what they were fighting for at the time. I was flabbergasted about how the city was responding to their situation. We were in court supporting Move 9 for weeks.

Every day was a different day with more eye-opening events. On this particular day, the judge allowed the proceedings to run long. This handsome young guy came to the courtroom that had never been there before. He seemed rather interested in what was going on, and he also came to see someone that was working in the courtroom. After sitting for a while, he left the courtroom. My girlfriend and I left the courtroom to take our children to the bathroom. We always walked together in groups for safety reasons.

NBA Rufus

As we were walking, the guy that was in the courtroom kept looking back at us. Then he asked, "Can I ask y'all a question?" We both laughed.

He asked questions about the Move organization because he was so intrigued about the organization. He asked us our names, and he told us his name was Rufus. He told us he was home from college for the summer, and he wanted to know more about the organization. I invited him to come over to our house, and he came that night. We sat outside and laughed and talked to him for hours that night. He asked if he could call me sometimes, and I said yes. I gave him the number, but I told him that I was only home during the evening.

He started coming over every evening because that time worked for both of us. He said he was in basketball training all day, so evenings were good for him. Well, as it turned out, he did not have basketball training; he had a girlfriend. But the time worked for both of us. We were together the entire summer, and it was so much fun. It was a summer fling, but at the end of the fling, I was pregnant. I didn't tell him right away because I could not believe I was pregnant by Rufus.

Move people were so happy for me, but I was not so happy. I was not in a place to bring another child into the world. Besides, Rufus was just supposed to be a fling, not a long-term relationship. We were living in two different worlds, and I was now a Move Supporter and a revolutionary. I had decided that I was going to be a part of changing how the world was run.

So You're Having My Baby

Rufus called me one day, and I told him that I was pregnant and he was shocked. I don't know how he was shocked when we slept together every night for a whole summer. He told me he was going to come home from school, but he didn't. I did not see Rufus until he came home for Christmas break. I was alone while carrying my baby, but I had the support of the entire Move Organization.

My experience while pregnant was the best. I ate a very clean diet, I ran every morning, and I exercised the entire pregnancy. I decided that I was going to deliver my baby at home like the Move women. Move people tried to convince me to have my baby at the hospital. They did not want me to feel any pressure or like I had to have my baby at home because that's something they did. But I was not changing my mind. I prepared for one of the most beautiful times in my life. No one could convince me to go to the hospital to have my baby. It was set in stone. I would have a home delivery all-natural.

During that time, I was alone, and a guy from the organization named Rick reached out to me. He was in prison with the other Move members. He was attracted to me, and he thought I was amazing. He loved my strength, my personality, and my no-nonsense happy-go-lucky attitude. He told me he had heard so much about me and was amazed to hear I was delivering my baby at home.

We started talking every day, and he was my main support system. He would call and encourage me always to be positive because he wanted the baby to pick up on positive and healthy energy. I fell in love with him due to the care and attention he had given me. I stopped going out to do things with the Move Supporters because I was getting really close to having my baby. I would stay home, and people were home with me in case I went into labor. I woke up one morning, and I felt really uncomfortable, but I was scared to let anyone know that I was feeling funny.

OMG, I was in labor, and I didn't even know it. Rick called me, and we were on the phone all day. He was so sweet and funny. He kept laughing and teasing me because I said I am not going to the hospital no matter how strong the pains got. He talked me through the labor, and he was allowed to stay on the phone with me into the wee hours of the night. It was a beautiful night, and my baby was coming tonight. The pain got stronger and stronger. I had the room prepared to give birth on a bed of hay. The atmosphere was so peaceful. I was naked, and I laid on the hay and gave birth to a beautiful baby girl. She was so cute and calm. She was absolutely amazing.

The moon was the light in my room, and the moment was so serene. After she came out, I was so tired that I fell asleep for a few moments. Then I pushed out the placenta and the after birth. I bit the cord with my teeth and held my beautiful baby on my chest. I could not put her down. I cleaned her up and laid her on my skin. We had skin-to-skin contact. It was the most beautiful thing in the world. I quickly forgot about the pain from the labor. I named her after Rick because he was there for her and me. The two people in the room with me were there to help me as midwives.

I had never had a baby naturally without going to the hospital before. They documented the time of my baby's birth, the date, her length, and weight. That experience was simply amazing. God was definitely in the room with me. He carried me through the entire experience. Thanks be to God who gives us the victory! Rufus came to see me, and he was seemingly happy, but he hadn't told his parents he would be a father.

Rufus stayed with me the entire time he was home, just like the summer, and then he disappeared again. After I had my baby, I did not call my mother right away because I was so exhausted. I waited until the next day when I had a little more strength. One of the ladies at my birth called my mother and said congratulations, your daughter had the baby earlier this morning. My mother was livid. She said, "Put my daughter on the phone now, please."

When I got on the phone, I was still pretty weak and exhausted, and my mother could hear that. She asked me what hospital I was at and why I had some bum calling her phone. She said, "I don't know them people."

My mother was always so sarcastic, and she didn't care who's feelings she hurt while being sarcastic. I answered and said that I was not in the hospital. I had the baby at home. Why did I say that?

My mother exploded. She lost it. My mother said, "WHAT! You had the baby at home?"

I said yes, and she just went in on me and cussed me out. She said, "you don't know anything about having a baby at home; you are not a doctor. You let those people talk you into doing something that you don't have any experience doing. You could have died having that baby. You could have hemorrhaged and died. You could have an infection right now that you don't know about. You are killing me right now. I have to go and take my heart medicine before I have a heart attack. I will talk to you later."

My mother hung up the phone. I was so embarrassed that the people had to witness all of that. I could not say a word in response because I was so weak, and I also reverted back to that little girl that would get a beating for being bad. The people in the house laughed and told me to let what my mother was saying go. They told me to be present in the beautiful moment of giving birth to my new baby girl, and I did just that.

The next day I went back to the house I lived in with two other Move Supporters. My room was very peaceful. I didn't have curtains on the windows, so the sunlight and the moonlight gleaned in the windows. It was serene, calm, and tranquil. I loved being there, and my children were at peace too. My new baby was so calm. She hardly ever cried. She was the best baby ever. She was perfect. I did not put clothes on her, and I held her most of the day. It was important to have skin-to-skin contact.

My oldest child was also so in love with the new baby. That was one of the best times in our lives. It was like being in heaven. It seemed like we had no worries. We all laid on the hay with the baby for a week. The hay was different, but I loved identifying with Jesus' birth. But soon, those tranquil moments would be interrupted by my mother. She came down to the house where I lived. My mother wanted to make sure that I, the baby, and my first daughter were okay. She needed to see me and lay her eyes on me to ensure I was okay after having the baby at home. My mother came to the house with her girlfriend, and she told me to bring the baby outside because she was not coming inside that house. The baby didn't have any clothes, so I wrapped the baby up in a big blanket really well. When my mother saw the baby, she started to cry. She was in awe that I had her at home and that the baby was absolutely beautiful. My mother called me every day to check on my children and me.

The Plan

I t wasn't long before my mother had a plan to get me away from the Move Supporters house. I didn't even know she was planning this move. She hooked up with Rufus and got him to bring the children and me over for the day. My mother and Rufus started to talk every day. Both of them had the same agenda, to get me to leave the Move organization. I felt different because when I was in need, MOVE people were there to help me. Move people were good to me, and Move people are great people. They catered to me while I was pregnant. I did not want for anything while I was pregnant with my second baby. However, my oldest daughter needed to go to school, and the Move children didn't go to school. They were all home-schooled.

When my mother talked to me about my daughter's need to go back to school in the fall, I was all in. So it wasn't hard to convince me to leave the organization and move back home. Rufus was happy, too, because he wanted to take the baby to see his family. When I moved back home, I was breastfeeding my baby, and she didn't have any clothes. My mother did not like the sight of me pulling out my breast to feed the baby. She would always say you are acting dirty like those people you lived with. She never embraced me breastfeeding my baby. It was a thing in her house. She went out and bought my baby Similac milk, bottles, and clothes. She didn't just buy clothes;

she bought my baby her first wardrobe. My mother was also bummed because she felt like nobody knew my baby was in the world. My mother said the world doesn't have any documentation that the baby is born.

My mother was very adamant about getting my daughter her proper documents. My mother didn't stop until she got my baby a birth certificate and a social security number. We lived with my mother, and she was so happy we were there. She felt like she rescued us from the Move organization. I was partly sad because I wanted to be with Rick, but he didn't want to talk to me again after leaving with Rufus. I always felt like I let the love of my life go in order to do what was right for my family. I was not willing to not send my children to school, and there were other philosophies that I just did not understand. I was not yet twenty-one years old. I still had some growing up to do.

Miz Melanie's Moments:
This is a really important fact to focus on. I had so much drama, hurt, and pain that I was carrying around, and I wasn't even twenty-one years old yet. I had lived a life full of trauma, drama, hurt, and pain, and I had not even become legal according to the world's principles. But yet I was loaded down with stuff, heavy stuff. This is how things pile upon us, one right after another. And if you don't know how to release or unpack these things, they will pile upon you, and you will carry them into other situations. Sometimes the stuff that we are carrying gets so heavy that we have a breakdown. And some

breakdowns are hard to come back from. Some people never recover from the heavy burdens and baggage we pile up in our lives. For example: Have you ever seen a homeless person with a lot of bags and stuff? They carry their things around with them everywhere they go. Afraid to put their bags down. This baggage has become a part of their lives, and it weighs on them over the years.

You can see their pain and hurt when you see them because they carry it around with them. Here's another example. When you break up from a relationship with your significant other, you should give yourself time to heal, deprogram yourself and just spend time releasing things that you don't want to bring into your next relationship. Focusing on yourself, regrouping, looking at yourself and things that you didn't like about yourself that that relationship brought out of you before you are ready for the next relationship. But sometimes, we meet someone and take all of our baggage from the prior relationship into the new relationship with the new person, and we start to feel like we are still in the same relationship. We are; it's just with a different person because we did not give ourselves time to heal. We just jumped into another relationship. Probably because we are lonely, or maybe for sex, or maybe because we want to show the other person who we just got out of a relationship with that we have moved on. All of these things are detrimental to our health. We just

add more stuff on top of the other stuff that we did not get rid of. We have to release the stuff, the baggage because it will eventually kill us.

I was finally all moved in with my mother. She was happy that I was home too. My mother was on the phone with her sisters and her girlfriend, telling them everything she bought for the baby. My mother was so happy that she rescued her daughter and her grandchildren. My mother and Rufus became close because she could talk to me through him. My mother allowed him to be at the house with me and the children, almost twenty-four seven.

When My Mother Leaves,
You Got To Leave

Then things started to get tight. Rufus was over at my mother's house the first thing in the morning and the last thing at night. If you know my mother, she doesn't like people sleeping in her house when she gets up and goes to work. And she doesn't like to leave a bunch of working-age people in her house when she goes to work. My mother started getting irritable in the mornings, and she started voicing her dislikes about the children and me. Then she said, "I don't want to have to trip over Rufus every damn time I come into my house."

I was baffled because she was so fond of him when she wanted him to do something for her. But she was ready for us to leave. My mother would allow me to come back home to get on my feet, and then she would put me out again. This one morning, she was furious, and she was tired of me, my children, and Rufus being in her space. She called Big Momma and told her she was sending me over to her house. Then she called the police and told them to take me to my grandmother's house. My mother told me to get all of me and my the children's things because we were not coming back to her house.

When the police arrived, she opened the door and said "It's time for y'all to leave."

The police put my daughters and me in the back of the police wagon. The police put dead bodies and criminals in the back of the wagon. Out of all the things that my mother did, I couldn't believe she did this. She called the police on my daughters and me and had us transported to Big Momma's house in a police wagon. I vowed to never, ever speak to my mother again. This was an all-time low, and not only did she do this to me but my children. My new baby was a few months old, but that was her house, and she did not want us there anymore.

When I arrived at Big Momma's house, Big Momma was waiting for the girls and me at the door. It wasn't a pleasant welcome. Big Momma was really angry with me. She had had enough of me and my antics. Big Momma told me to get myself together, and she said if I think that she is going to let me and Rufus lay up in her house, we were sadly mistaken. Big Momma told me to feed those children, bathe them, get them dressed, and figure out what I would do with my life. I immediately knew that I had to get out of there. I was not and could not stay with Big Momma. That was going to drive me completely crazy.

Nowhere to Go

When Rufus came over that morning, the children and I got in his car and went to the park so that I could think. I decided to go to my Aunt Rachel's house. My Aunt Rachel, the person who discovered that I was pregnant by eavesdropping on my conversation with her son. I asked my aunt if we could stay over at her house, and she said yes. She said she needed some company. I was so happy that day. I was on cloud nine because I had somewhere to lay my head, and I wasn't under pressure because she seemed like she wanted me to be there more than I wanted to be there. However, there was a catch to staying there. My Aunt Rachel's house was filthy, clothes everywhere, junk everywhere.

Her house was small, cluttered and she was a hoarder. But Aunt Rachel was happy because she owned that house. I opted to sleep on the couch because that was the cleanest place in the entire house. I had to clean it up to fit my standards, especially the bathroom, but it was home for my children and me for now. She even allowed Rufus to stay the night when he wanted.

My aunt was the best. We both were sitting outside on her steps, and she asked me if my oldest daughter knew how to ride a bike. She went to the thrift store and bought my oldest daughter a bike without training wheels, and she taught her how to ride that bike. My daughter fell, and she told me to leave her alone, don't run to her rescue, let her get back on that bike, and learn how to ride it. Within hours my daughter knew how to ride a bike without training wheels. And she rode that little bike up and down the street all day long, every day. I was so relieved that I could put my burdens down for a minute and regroup.

My aunt loved Rufus, and she would sit him down and give him wisdom about life and taking care of the little family he created with me. She told Rufus that he had to step up to the plate and get a good job and housing for us. Rufus loved Aunt Rachel, and he valued her wisdom. That's a perk that I love about the hood. The older generation always gives the younger generation the real deal about being black in the hood and how to maneuver to get out of the hood.

One day Aunt Rachel came to me and told me she needed to talk to me. She told me that her son was being released from jail in a few weeks, and he had to come and stay at her house. She told me that he was in jail for molesting his girlfriend's daughters. She told me that she knows that he did it and that she wanted to let me know before he came home. She told me that I was more than welcome to stay at her house, but she had to tell me the truth.

Aunt Rachel told me that her son did molest his girlfriend's children and that she didn't want to put my children in the same predicament. She told me that if I wanted to get my own apartment that I had to go and stay at a shelter and that they would then get me an apartment within days. I discussed this option with Rufus, but I did not care what his response would be because he could go to his mother's house every night and sleep. I needed an apartment for my children and me.

The Salvation Army / The Shelter

I went and checked myself into the shelter (The Salvation Army). I had to stay in for a week (I could not leave the premises) to get processed. After the week, I had to get dressed, eat breakfast, and then talk to the social worker. The social/caseworker set up a plan to make sure I would maintain the apartment when I got it. I also had to give a portion of my welfare check to them to save to have a deposit to move into my apartment. I hated it there, but it was necessary for me to get my apartment. I did not want to be in the predicament of people telling me to get out of their house again. So, I endured the shelter experience to get my kids and me a home.

There were all kinds of people in the shelter. I was very uncomfortable being there, but I had no other way to get an apartment. We were at the shelter for about three weeks, and they said they had an apartment for me in the projects. I was so happy because I finally got my own place. I wished I could have been given a single home and not a project, but that was what they had, and I took it. The Lord has been with me all of my life, as you can see by now.

When I went to see the apartment, my uncle's mother-in-law worked in the office. God granted me favor. When you move in the projects according to the tenants' rules, you have to start from the top floor and work your way down when openings become available. However, because of the favor of God upon my life, even in the valley low place, I was able to get an apartment on the second floor. One flight of steps up. That was considered a luxury because you didn't have to take the elevator. The elevator always got stuck, smelled like pee, and was broken most of the time.

My apartment was the apartment over the entrance of the building, and everyone in the entire building wanted that apartment. I had people approach me when I first moved in to ask me how I got my apartment. Some lady even told me the rules for the apartment. She said "you are supposed to move to the top floors before qualifying for any apartments on the lower floors."

I was saying to myself, "And I don't care what the rules are. I am already in my new apartment."

It was really a thing because these people were mad at me for not starting on the seventeenth floor. Anyways I didn't allow that to bother me. The Salvation Army had given me vouchers to get furniture. I got a living room set, girls' beds, and a dresser for Rufus and me. Rufus moved in, and we were one big happy family. Rufus was a good-looking guy, and we had a great relationship, so I thought. But Rufus had a problem with the women. He did not know how to be in a relationship with a mature woman. I did not have time to play because I had two children, and I was ready to settle down and be a family.

Miz Melanie's Moments:
I have to give Rufus a pass here because he was a young man in college, and then he met me. His life

went from boys to men in a span of months. He did not have the responsibility of a family. He had no clue as to how to be the head of the household. I was the head of my household, the breadwinner, and everything in between. I already had a start at parenting, and he was just coming on board. We started unequally yoked. I was the only one who knew what the family needed and everything that needed to be done. It was my apartment, and I was in charge. When you go into a relationship like this, you are always going to have problems, because everything is out of order from the beginning. Rufus was never the man of the house. He was never made to feel like he set the order. I got the apartment, the welfare check, the food stamps, the medical card, so I had the last word. Do Not Ever start a relationship off like this. For women, if your significant other doesn't have more to offer in the situation, they are not the one.

When you start like this, you are doomed for disaster. Your significant other should have more to bring to the table to make the table set to eat. Meaning they should be bringing more to take the burden off of you. The relationship between Rufus and I was never going to survive because our situation was out of order from the beginning. We were unequally yoked from the beginning, and we did not have a plan. We put a plan in place down the road, but Rufus was unable to be Captain of the ship because he had issues that he brought to the relationship, and that is Rufus's story to tell.

`Rufus was a cheater, and he thought he was slick, but he can't slick a can of oil. I was on to him, and I didn't want to play those games with him. Because that was my apartment, I would tell him to get out when he would get caught. One day he left, and I was pissed because this other girl had told him to come and stay with her. But we were a family, and I wasn't going for that. I went and found him, and we got into a big fight. I left and went home. I thought he would meet me there, but he didn't.

I dressed in all black, and I drove around until I found his car. I did not know where the girl lived, but I knew he was not far behind when I found that car. I busted the car windows out and blew the horn until he woke up. I was calling out his name aloud, and all the neighbors were looking out the windows and in their doors. When he woke up because apparently, he was in the girl's house sleeping, he ran outside in tears because he could not believe that I had busted out his car windows.

After I saw he was hurt, I left the scene. He could not believe I had torn up his pride and joy. Rufus loved that car. He washed that car and fixed it every chance he got. He loved that car, and that car was his money maker. He made money giving people rides, and he did odd jobs too. He came over to my apartment the next day, and when I opened the door, he punched me right in the eye. He was mad, and so was I. We fought all day, and then we made up that night with make-up sex.

That was our routine. Every time we were in an argument or fight because we fought a lot, we would make up with sex. Until I had enough, I could no longer live this life of poverty, sadness, lack, heartbreak, and stagnation. I knew there was more to life for me. I knew the Lord had a plan for my life, and this was not it. I was not to get comfortable living this life.

One day I was out on my balcony looking over the entire neighborhood, and I heard the Lord loud and clear say to me that this is not what He has planned for me. He said, "Do not settle for this life. I have more for you."

At that point, I received the word, and I was on a quest to find out how to get out of this maze that I was in. I contacted my spiritual mother and told her what I was feeling. She prayed for me, and she sought the Lord on my behalf. She would pray for me until the Lord would send an answer. I thank God for putting her in my life. She still prays for me today. I love her, and God sent her when I needed him the most. She covered me in prayer and laid on the Lord for me when I was weak. To be honest, I was always weak. I did not know how to get rid of these burdens, and I did not know how to forgive or release the stuff I was carrying. God sent her to be a help in my time of need. Hallelujah!

I still give God praise when I think about the things that He has delivered me from. I needed a break from Rufus because I was exhausted from our relationship. I started hanging with Sabrina again. I saw them somewhere, and they all missed me, and I missed the family too. I started going over there every weekend and staying from Friday until Sunday.

I left Rufus right down there in the projects where he wanted to be. He had a chance to get a taste of his own medicine. I loved to spend time with Sabrina and her family because we were now just family. Her mother was my mother. Her sisters and brothers were my sisters and brothers. Everybody that knew them knew that I was one of the daughters. Mom Dee told me to move back home. "You were not brought up in those projects."

She hated when I would leave and go back on Sunday. But my children were in school from that address, so I had to go back on Sundays. I would be there for the week and prepare to go back to Mom Dee's house on Friday. I adored and admired Sabrina's oldest sister (Millie) because she loved my daughters and me. Millie would always talk to me about doing better for myself, and she would always try to help me better myself. Millie told me to move back home (Mom Dee's house) and get rid of Rufus because he is not doing anything to help me. Millie told me to come and work with her and our other sisters.

Private Dancer

Millie said, "Come and join the family business." They were doing good and making lots of money. They could make a few thousand dollars a week easy, and we were not selling drugs. I was all in. I had to come to a meeting with Millie, and she told me all about the job and what was required. She gave me the rules, the dos and the don'ts of the job. I was so ready to get started. I had to get uniforms and go to a second interview at the actual job site.

I was now in the dancer for money business. I had to go to this gentleman's bar and dance on the stage. I was paid for my interview as if it was a booking. I had some fear because I had never done this type of work before, but I was determined to make a few thousand dollars a week. I had heard all of the stories about what goes on in these places, how to stay safe, and what to do to be credible.

Now my moment of truth had come, and I was ready to get started. Millie had taken me out and bought me some outfits. The outfits were temporary until I could get a few outfits made. I arrived at my booking early because I wanted to scout out the land. When I arrived, I told the girl behind the bar that I was here to see the owner, John. She called him, and he came out to meet me.

He seemed like an upstanding businessman. He didn't seem like he would ask me to do anything that I did not want to do. He interviewed me and told me to get on the stage and do my thing. I got dressed, and the bartender asked me if I wanted a drink. At first, I thought it's too early for a drink, but she said "this will help your nerves."

I ordered a drink, and I got on the stage. The drink made me feel relaxed, and it enabled me to be sexy and seductive. The fear had almost evaporated, and I was dancing like a pro, or so I thought. After I finished my four-hour set, I had an evaluation review. This establishment that I was working in was known all over the city for businessmen, city officials, lawyers, and even judges frequent John's spot. This place had a good reputation, and the men that came there were regulars with big money.

In my evaluation, the owner John told me that I was a good dancer, I had the men engaged, and they were spending money, but I needed to get some real uniforms. He told me that I had on lingerie, and he doesn't allow lingerie on his stage. He said I had to get the correct uniform to get booked on his rosters. I was kind of embarrassed by what he said because he was a man about business and business only. I could not use my charm on him because his demeanor was stoic. He called Millie and told her my review, and she was a little softer when she and I talked about my first day on the stage. I ordered about seven outfits because I was now an official dancer for money. That phrase comes from Tina Turner's Private Dancer song.

Millie was a booking agent, and she booked dancers for different venues. Of course, she would book her sisters first, and we all were working all the time. We had consistent work almost seven days a week. Millie had a good upstanding reputation in the dance world. The men knew to respect her, and her dancers and the people she booked with knew she was reliable, dependable, and all business. She did not play about her or her staff's money. If you booked her or her people for a job, pay them their money. Also, she did not fraternize with the customers. Millie's motto was, do your job, get your money and get out of the place. If you want a drink or to hang out, don't do it where you work. You never play where you work.

Millie started off booking me jobs with her to show me the ropes and introduce me around to everyone she knew so they would put extra protection on me when I had to work by myself. At the end of every shift, the bouncer or security would walk us to the cars. We tipped them because we appreciated the extra protection. Millie always booked all of us together. It was like a family trip every day, and that helped me a lot. I felt secure being with my family. We would meet at Mom Dee's every day, get our snacks, drinks, weed, and get on the road.

Millie didn't drink or smoke; she was all business and the designated driver. We had a great reputation in the dance world. Every place that had dancers called and requested Millie and her sisters. We were always working a few gigs a day. I would be tired as hell when I would get home, but I did not come home with less than $700.00 a night. And $700.00 was a slow night. We did not have to do anything strange for some change either. However, there were girls on the job that did, and those chicks made thousands of dollars every night.

I often wanted to do what they were doing for the money because I could use all the money I could get. I was a single parent, and I was used to living a certain way. I did not like living in the projects after Rufus and I did not work out. I bought a new car, got a new apartment, and bought cream furniture for my living room.

I was a boss making boss moves. My entire apartment was newly furnished, and my children had everything that they wanted. I was living the life, or so I thought. I started getting requests for bookings. I was making good money and driving a nice car. I met men that were very generous to me. They would give me whatever I asked for because they wanted to say that I was dating them. I was dancing from Philadelphia to New York City. But the work had its dangerous times too.

One night I was working with my sisters, and this man was giving me all of his money for lap dances. He went to the mac machine and came back with more money for me. I had a trademark phrase that we would all laugh about on the way home every night. I would tell all of those men that I loved them while giving them a lap dance. I told this one man that I loved him, and he kept asking me, "Do you really love me?"

I would say, "Yes, baby. I love you."

He would pull out more money and just give it to me. I gave him my number because I wanted to get every dime that he had if I could. He was a guy that I could manipulate for his money. I didn't have to give up any booty because I could talk a good game with this particular type of guy.

On this particular night, it was time to pay up. I guess I had taken him to his peak, and he wanted me to give him what I promised him. He kept watching me all night, and he started begging me to let him sleep with me that night. I told him that I had to go with my sisters and pick up my children. He would not take no for an answer. So, when we left the bar to go home, we noticed that he was following us. That man followed us from New Brunswick, New Jersey, to Philly.

We were all in the car scared because I had told him that I could not sleep with him that night. I hadn't planned to sleep with him ever, I was just playing with his emotions, and he was serious. We were so scared that we drove to the police station and told the police that the man was following us from New Brunswick, New Jersey. The police got involved and detained him while they let us drive off. We laugh about it now, but he could have killed my sisters and me because of my stupidity.

Miz Melanie's Moments:

Be careful how you treat people. I mistreated this man, and I was playing with his feelings and emotions. I targeted him because I knew that he was hungry for someone to love him, care about him and spend time with him. I took complete advantage of him and his kindness. He did all of those things for me, giving me all of his money because he was hoping for something more, and I knew that. I was able to find out that he had a good job and he had a few dollars. But he wasn't the kind of guy that I would be caught with. I treated him like men were treating me that I wanted that did not want me. It was the same behavior that was inflicted on me that I was inflicting on someone else. I did not like to be unwanted and overlooked or treated like a one-night stand. But yet, I was treating this man that was not popular with the women the exact same way. That's why he was in the bar trying to get his rocks off with the sexy women on the stage. I had become what I despised, a user and manipulator. Please be careful how you treat people because you never know who the person you are mistreating is. Hebrews 13:2 / Ephesians 4:32

I had some days that I considered good days. I met a man that absolutely loved me, and I loved him too. But he had a girlfriend that he was serious about, and they had just had a baby. He was older, and the girl was young like me, but she didn't want him. She wanted him for what he could do for her.

On the other hand, I really liked him, and I would have stopped dancing to be with him. That's how much I loved him. He bought me a car, and he was very generous with his money. I also met an African man that I was intrigued with. He was a very accomplished man, an accountant in Princeton, New Jersey. Princeton is a well-accomplished community where the elite lived. He was well known in the community, and he was always well dressed. He would send some of the girls to Nigeria to transport money. He would tape the money on their bodies with tape, and they would wear girdles to carry the money safely on their bodies and wear jackets and coats to camouflage that they were carrying the money. They would get paid ten thousand dollars each trip, and some of the girls stopped dancing to take trips transporting money to Nigeria.

He never told me about the money trips the girls did. I wanted him to send me so badly so I could make that kind of money in one trip. I never considered that they could not just turn around and come back after they delivered the money. They had to stay in Nigeria for at least two weeks to make it look like a vacation or trip. I didn't consider the consequences if I got caught with the money. I just wanted to get out of the living paycheck to paycheck life. I just wanted to be well off; money ain't a problem type of living without working hard.

This African guy just wanted me to look good on his hip, and I did. But I felt something wasn't right with this love connection. He had a daughter that was thirsty to come over to my house and spend the night with my daughters. Her mother was in Nigeria, and he wanted an American mother for his daughter. I felt like I would be hooked up in something that would have been hard for me to get out of. I did not know exactly what he was up to, so I started to distance myself from him.

I started not answering his calls, and eventually, he stopped calling. I also met an Italian guy obsessed with black women, but there was also something strange about him. He owned a Lil Caesar's pizza shop, and he said he was also a bounty hunter. At first, I was excited because he owned his own business, but things started to get strange. He would bring me envelopes filled with cash, and if I was not at home, he would leave them under my door.

He told me sometimes he would just come and sit parked outside of my apartment and just watch to see what kind of action was going on in my neighborhood. That made me feel weird about him. Every Monday, he would take me on a date, and this particular Monday, he said we would do something special. He took me down Penn's Landing, and we went to a helipad where he chartered a helicopter. I thought he was taking me on a helicopter ride and I was terrified. But we were going there for his helicopter lessons.

When I told my mother that I was seeing this Italian guy that owned a pizza shop, was a bounty hunter, and took helicopter lessons, she freaked out. She told me to leave him alone because I was playing with fire. My mother told me that he was probably a hitman and a drug supplier. She said that's why he is taking those helicopter lessons. My mother said he was learning how to transport the drugs from New York to Philly. I was really freaked out after she told me that. I just subtly removed myself from him by being super busy. I had to get out of there while I had a chance because I didn't want to be caught up in his stuff.

Secret Lovers

Then, I fell into a situation with this younger guy who admired me, and I had no idea. He was hanging around my best friend and me. We would get together every Sunday to go out to eat or a movie. One day he asked me to come over to his house because he needed my advice on something. I went over to see him after work to help him with whatever it was that he needed help with.

When I arrived, he told me he needed to tell me something first. He said "I have admired you from the first day that I met you. You're a great person, and deserve to be treated like a queen."

He told me that I was doing a great job raising my children, and he wanted to appreciate me. He had cooked me a steak dinner with potatoes, a salad, and biscuits. He had a carrot cake and ice cream for dessert. He had wine, beer, and weed. He had soft love music playing, and he had prepared a bath to bathe me. I was stunned because I didn't know he was looking at me like that. I sure wasn't looking at him like that. But that day, I received all of the appreciation.

He kissed me and then started to undress me. He bathed me and caressed my entire body. I was wowed by his love language and how he executed the entire evening. He massaged me from head to toe, and that was amazing.

I was dazed because when you are a single mother, you wear so many hats constantly. It seems like you never get a break, and for me to get this much-needed TLC was absolutely what the doctor ordered. I needed to be held by a man, and I needed to feel wanted, and I needed to be catered to by a man. I needed to release all of my burdens and exhale, and it felt amazing. We ate dinner, smoked weed, drank wine, slow danced, kissed, laughed, made love, talked, dreamed, held each other, and were in love at that moment.

He made crazy love to me. He seemingly took away all of my cares in those hours. I did not want to leave that moment because all of the things I wanted were wrapped up at that moment. He planned a great evening. However, our relationship changed that day. We were no longer friends; we were lovers. Every woman wants a man to plan this kind of moment for both of them together. That evening was magical, and an evening I always dreamed of. That evening was an evening that every single mother needs to experience. It was everything. It was an evening of love, and I loved every moment of it. I wished I could have an evening like that every month.

Miz Melanie's Moments:
That kind of release is needed for a single mother to balance out life's circumstances. We have to navigate everything for our family, and life can get really hard. Single mothers have so much to deal with on a day-to-day basis. Every single mother needs to have some time with a man to take the

weight off of their shoulders. This needs to be the start of something new on your schedule. Self-care doesn't only consist of pampering yourself at the spa, buying new clothes, shoes, bags, and vacationing. Self-care is also releasing yourself. You need to be made love to, passionate love, to give you balance. We need that to center us. God told Adam to make love to his wife. Be fruitful and multiply. It's essential for our well-being as women. Being single just makes it complicated, and we don't have access to a partner like God-ordained.

Work Hard For The Money

I continued to go to work. I was booked and busy, but I had to leave my children home alone sometimes. I thank God that He watched over them while I was gone letting no weapon formed against me prosper because the devil was lurking. I would go to work and call my daughters at every stop. I would be parenting from the phone. My routine or schedule was to either make sure that they were over my mother's house or have everything they needed before I would leave. If they were over at my mother's house, I could breathe a sigh of relief. But if I had to leave them home alone, I had to call every hour or when I got my break to give directions over the phone. But mommy had to work because we needed the money, and daddy was doing his own thing.

Taking care of the children was not one of the things that daddy was doing at that time. So I did not complain too much. I just did the job given to me. I did the job the best way that I knew how. I was not given a manual at the beginning of motherhood, so I was learning on-the-job training as I went. This gig of motherhood is the most important job in the world. Motherhood can bring you the most beautiful times in your life, but it's the hardest job in the world.

I developed my prayer life due to becoming a mother. I prayed and prayed and prayed all of my children's lives and still praying. I would go to work and come in late at night with a suitcase full of money. I would buy food, toys, and books for my youngest daughter to keep her occupied, and I would buy clothes, shoes, bags, and money in her wallet for my oldest.

That's my material girl, and she loved to go shopping. I always rewarded her because she was stepping in helping where she was not supposed to. She was helping me with the day-to-day of the family. My oldest daughter was and still is a great help to me. I always pray that God Blesses her Abundantly because she has a heart of pure gold. I always love to dance for older men because they are more mature. Most older men that came to the places that I dance at knew how to treat the girls. They knew all of the girls, and we had a rapport with them. So I was very comfortable in every place I went because I knew somebody would be there to look out for me.

On the other hand, I hated dancing for younger guys because first of all, they didn't have money to spend. Younger guys would come to the bar and nurse a drink all night and one dollar you all night. Older men spent that money. When younger guys that had money like the drug dealers, they would be super nasty. They did not understand the concept of the dancer. A dancer's job in a gentlemen's club is seductively entertaining men, giving them fantasy, and performing lap dances if the establishment requires that. But for me, younger guys aren't mature enough to enjoy just watching and not touching.

I watch the girls today, and that's nothing like what I was doing. I did not show my breast or my vagina. We had to wear uniforms. They could be provocative, but we had to have something covering our breast and vagina. Pasties were permitted in some places. On one Saturday, I was booked to do a party for these young guys, and I really wanted to turn the job down, but the money was great. The person who was given the party was paying $150.00 an hour plus tips. I was booked for three hours, but I could work later if money was flowing. So, I estimated that I would make at least $500 or $600 for the afternoon.

I only planned to stay a total of 4-5 hours because it was Saturday, and I needed to be home to spend some time with my daughters. The event started at 11:00, and it was scheduled to end around 6:00 or 7:00 that evening. When I first started dancing, it was empty in the place. I was cool because I thought this job would be a get-in and get-out real quick gig. Then the guys started to come in, and they had a little bit of money, but they wanted to almost have sex in the lap dance for the money. I was so over this event, and I was ready to go home.

The guys were young and silly, and they were getting on my nerves. The crowd was like a fraternity crowd of guys, drinking and acting stupid. I was dancing on one of my sets on the floor, and this one guy in the crowd had one drink too many. He came on the floor and put out a cigarette on my butt. I lost my mind at that moment. I said, "You ugly mother fucker, you don't know what your mother had to do to feed your ugly ass," and I walked off of the floor.

At first, he was laughing and acting stupid. But some of the other guys who were there started taking up for me and cussing him out. The guy who booked the event came running to the dressing room to see if he could resolve the issue, but I was pissed off. I felt so humiliated at that moment. I was crying and disappointed with myself for being in that predicament. I got dressed, and I left the event.

Miz Melanie's Moments:
I was bleeding profusely inside from this wound. I had hit rock bottom. I had hit a brick wall. I could not go any further. I needed my Father. I didn't have access to my biological father, but I could always reach my Heavenly Father. My Abba Father was always there knocking on the door of my heart, waiting to come deeper into my heart. Jesus promised never to leave or forsake me. So I knew I could go to him. I knew the Lord was my safe place. I knew he would take really good special care of me. I knew Jesus would be there. I needed to get in Jesus ' lap, and I needed Him to hold me in His arms. The Hand of the Lord was always on my life! Hallelujah! Thank You, Jesus!

I Cried Out To The Lord

I drove to the park, and I cried, and I talked to God. This was a hard conversation because I wanted to know why am I a single parent? I also told God that I was doing this to help keep a roof over me and my children's heads. I had so many questions that I dare not ask God before. When I left that booking, that was my last day dancing. I was belittled, demeaned, humiliated, ashamed, mortified, embarrassed, degraded, and more. I felt like the bottom of his shoe. I made a vow to myself that nobody is ever going to treat me like that again.

For days after that, I laid before the Lord in prayer and cried. I needed washing and cleansing. I went back to church. I joined a prayer band with some washed, cleansed, purified women of God. We prayed every Monday evening, and I also leaned on my spiritual mother, who nursed me back to health. I could not believe I had been treated like that by that guy. He was the unattractive guy, the ugly guy, out of the bunch, and he wanted to be funny, but the joke didn't go over right with the guys he was with.

Some of the guys there apologized for what that guy did, and a few of them asked me to stay. But I was mortified and embarrassed at that moment, and I could not face them after that. That guy that put that cigarette out on my butt had already treated me like trash on the street. My career as a private dancer, dancer for money, ended at that moment. I repented for my sins, and I wrapped myself up in the arms of Jesus. I was wounded and needed some TLC from my Heavenly Father.

Decisions, Decisions, Decisions

Every day we have to make decisions, decisions, and more decisions. We decide when we wake up how we will handle the day's events. It's one decision after another. Good decisions and some bad decisions. But, the point that I am making is, we make decisions all day, every day. When God put Adam and Eve in the garden, He gave them their own will. God told them that they could eat whatever they wanted, But they could not eat from the tree of knowledge, the tree of good and evil. Genesis 2:16-17.

At that point, God had given them their own mind. God had allowed them to make their own decisions. God has also given us the same power to make our own decisions. It's up to us to make the right decisions. Because they ate the fruit from the tree of good and evil, we now have to decide whether we will make the right decision or the wrong decision. At times we make the wrong decision because of the state of mind that we are in at the time of the decision.

Never make a life decision when you are angry or upset. You tend to make the wrong decision because of your state of mind at the time of the decision. The devil loves for us to make a decision when we are going through a crisis or when we are desperate because it is easy for him to manipulate our minds when we are in that state of mind. There are a lot of people in prison, on drugs, or even dead because of decisions made while desperate or while they were upset.

I Decided Tooooooooooooooooo
I have decided to live my life honestly and in truth. I have decided to turn my hurt, pain, and sins into my triumph, my testimony! I decided never to let anyone mistreat me again. I decided not to allow anyone to abuse me again. I decided not to let anyone dump their stuff on me. I decided to get free of all the things that were trying to kill me, destroy me, and steal everything I have.

I decided to release all of the stuff that I was carrying around all of my life. I decided to empty all of the old baggage that had piled up in my life. I decided to dance and replace all of that sadness, hurt, and pain with Joy. I decided to let go of all the negative stuff attached to my heart, and the ugliness hiding in my heart. I decided to unpack all of the accumulated baggage over the years since I was molested and raped. I decided to take ownership for the things I have done wrong and the mistakes I have made. I decided to cleanse my mind of all the terrible things that I was thinking about myself. I decided to ask you to forgive me. I decided to forgive. I decided to forgive myself. I decided to love me. I decided to laugh and enjoy my life. I decided to believe God! I decided to LIVE.

What have you decided to do today? I pray that you decide to get free and LIVE! Today is the day to make the right decisions for your life. I don't care what situation that you find yourself in. You could be in prison, sick, on drugs, an alcoholic, a prostitute, a child molester, whatever you are struggling with, decide to change your situation around now. Start today and get healed, delivered, and set free! Look that stuff that you are carrying right in the face and tell that stuff that you lived your last day with me yesterday. Unpack all of those bags that you have accumulated over the years. Stuff has gravitated to you because of the state that you were in. But God wants to remove all of the negative and cleanse your heart, body, soul, and mind. Don't wait until tomorrow; make the decision today to LIVE!

Looking At Things From My View

Parents, mothers, fathers, single parents, especially single mothers. I want you to know that you are the very first teacher in your children's life. Everything that we as parents do, be it good or bad, our children are watching and learning. If you as a parent are an avid reader, you teach your child to read and make reading mandatory in your household; your child will most likely be a reader. If you drink all of your child's life, it's more than likely that your child will be a drinker. My point is children are impressionable, and they mimic what they see.

This book is from my view as a child. How we as parents mean something is not how things are often downloaded and translated to our children. We have to talk to our children. We must explain things to our children because their capacity for understanding is predicated on their age. Our children are our babies, and we are their first love. That means we must be careful what they digest, what they consume, and how they develop. It's hard work, but it's rewarding to see the manifestation of the work you put in.

We, as parents, are not perfect, but to our children, we are; therefore, we have a responsibility to let them know that we too make mistakes. Let them know that's why we don't want them to repeat the mistakes that we made. We want our children to be the best version of themselves by avoiding the landmines that we fell prey to. Let your children know when they have done good and make it a priority to celebrate them. Also, correct them when they do something wrong. Talk to them after they have been corrected for doing something wrong and let them verbalize what they were thinking at that moment. Don't talk at them, don't talk down to them, allow them to have a voice.

Correction is good because it teaches life lessons. Those lessons will be with them all of their lives. When you punish your child after the punishment, have a sit-down talk with your child and explain why the punishment was necessary for their actions. Tell them that it's important that they get this lesson now so they won't have to learn a harder lesson later in life. Communication is essential for a relationship with your child. Teach them that they are the most beautiful person in the world inside and outside. Build up their confidence at home so that they won't have to look for validation outside in the streets. The street version of validation is not the validation that they want or need.

The streets often offer our children compromise, and that compromise might cost them their life. These are our children, a gift given to us personally from God, Himself. So we must love them, cherish them, and give them the necessary ingredients to make good decisions. We can raise great healthy, loving, confident, achieving children. But we must be willing to use the tools given to us by the Lord, and the main tool is prayer. Prayer changes things, prayer makes things happen, prayer will open your eyes and allow you to see things that you never knew about, prayer brings you into the room with God Almighty, Our Lord, and

Savior. Prayer is a necessity when you are raising children. ***Prayer saved my life. Prayer is Essential!***

My Mother

My mother was the best mother that she knew how to be due to the circumstances. She wanted the best for her children. Did she make some mistakes? Yes, but she did the job to the best of her ability. My mother had stuff, unpacked baggage that she never unpacked. Those things interfered with her ability to be greater in life. Due to my mother's wounds, my mother was unable to raise me without major scars. We all want the best for our children, and we all start that way, but sometimes things and circumstances get in the way. My mother is now deceased, and I am saddened that I could not unpack my stuff, my issues, my hurts, and my pain before she departed this life.

I am sad that I could not verbally voice with a clear mind and forgiving heart in a sit-down conversation with my mother. As I reminisce on my mother's many accomplishments, I now realize that my mother was an incredible woman. My mother was a mother and a father simultaneously, and my mother was a leader. My mother was a civil rights leader and the President of a great union for state workers. My mother fought for people's jobs and their rights. My mother was a secretary; my mother was a college student; my mother was an executive. My mother was a hustler and a businesswoman. My mother was a great sister, daughter, and friend. My mother was a beautiful person. My mother was an awesome chef. My mother was a disciplinarian, a mover, and a shaker. My mother got things done. My mother was a great example of the things she was great at. My mother loved to help others. My mother was scorned, broken, and hurt.

We never talked about this, but I believe my mother was raped, too. My mother was a phenomenal woman! I now understand my mother, and I will forever love my mother. My mother had to wear so many hats, and some stuff fell through the cracks. I fell through the cracks. Somebody dropped me at birth, and I had some bruises, and at times I was lame; I could not walk or talk due to the things I endured. Sometimes Jesus had to carry me because I was too weak and feeble to stand on my own two feet. Just like Mephibosheth. (2 Samuel verse 9) Jesus had someone carry me to the King's table, and now I sit, and I eat because...I Am Royalty!

If you are a victim of childhood sexual abuse, sexual abuse, physical abuse, mental abuse, drug abuse, domestic violence, or if you are feeling suicidal, please call these numbers for HELP!
Childhood Sexual Abuse / Sexual Abuse Hotline
RAINN --- 800-656-4673
Drug and Alcohol Abuse Hotline 1-800-662-4357
Suicide Prevention Hotline 800-273-8255
Domestic Violence Hotline 800-799-7233

Heavenly Father, in the name of Jesus Christ Your Son, I thank You for Your grace, Your mercy, Your love, and Your forgiveness. You have freed me from the yokes and bondages of this world.

Father, You have set my feet upon a rock and established my goings. You have equipped me with the tools necessary to open locked doors. You have released me from every generational curse and taught me how to cleanse my mind from every worry, every hindrance, and every roadblock that would try to plague my life.

Father, You have taught me how to release every burden that attached itself to me. Father, You have gone before me and made every crooked place in my life straight. You have released me from every prison that kept me bound and feeling worthless. Father, you have shown me the love that I have been searching for all of my life, and because of You, I am free! In Jesus' name, Amen

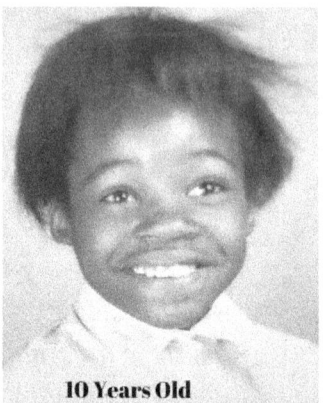

**10 Years Old
When the Abuse started**

15 Years Old

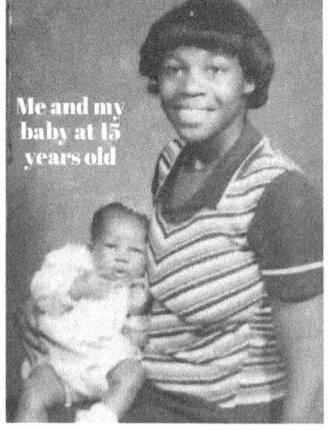

Me and my baby at 15 years old

I Am FREE!

I DECIDED
TO LAUGH!

163

About

Melanie Stroman

Melanie Stroman is a Philadelphia native currently residing in Los Angeles California.

She is the Mother to three beautiful talented daughters. She enjoys reading, writing, traveling, dancing, listening to music, and helping others see the brighter side of things.

She is a Certified Life Coach, Motivational Speaker and her life work is to help others recognize and release hurts from the past.

Melanie decided a few years ago to release the

baggage of her past and start laughing. She believes laughter is medicine for the soul.

Her prescription for everyday life is to Release, Laugh, Live and Enjoy life.

To Book MJ STROMAN Please send an email to mizmelaniebooks@gmail.com

Instagram   @mizmelaniebooks
Twitter   @BookMizMelanie
Facebook   Miz Melanie Books

www.ingramcontent.com/pod-product-compliance
Lightning Source LLC
Chambersburg PA
CBHW060524130626

46553CB00002B/646